We Waved to the Baker

By the same author:

Footsteps in the Furrow

We Waved to the Baker
Tales of a rural childhood

Andrew Arbuckle

Illustrated by Graham Lang

Old Pond Publishing Ltd

Published by
Old Pond Publishing Ltd
Dencora Business Centre,
36 White House Road, Ipswich, IP1 5LT,
United Kingdom

Cover design by Liz Whatling
Typesetting by Galleon Typesetting, Ipswich
Printed and bound in Malta

Contents

Dedication

To John, Willie and Gina
who shared in these adventures

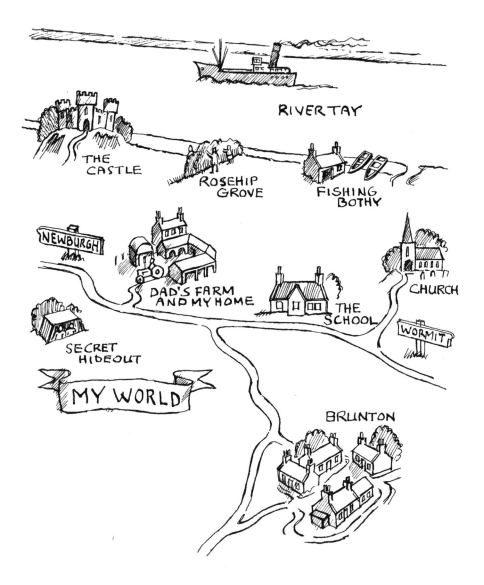

RIVER TAY

THE CASTLE

ROSEHIP GROVE

FISHING BOTHY

NEWBURGH

DAD'S FARM AND MY HOME

THE SCHOOL

CHURCH

WORMIT

SECRET HIDEOUT

MY WORLD

BRUNTON

Two Views from a Window

TODAY, as I sit down in my chair by the window, the river is full, sluggish and slow. That is its present mood. Over the past sixty years, I have watched the River Tay put on many different performances. It may be Scotland's largest river, but on the lowest of tides it shows off its undergarments, the many sand and mud banks, as if some great sea god has pulled the plug. Then with a change of moon and tide, it can look massive and majestic, lipping over onto the rich farmland along its banks. I once farmed that land and so I recognise the truth spoken by a king of Scotland that this narrow strip of land between the river and the hills behind is a 'fringe of gold' around Fife. I see the fields where, before my working life, my father tilled the land with the large number of workers that were needed for the hardworking farming that existed half a century ago.

I close my eyes a little more and, slipping back into the softness of the armchair, distance myself from the immediate issues of my day. Daydreaming is one of the joys of life and I have at least sixty years of experience in doing just that, quietly closing the rest of the world off and thinking my own thoughts.

Today I see a small gaggle of school children walking along the quiet country road in front of my house. The road connects the farms that lie along the fertile strip of land bounded in the north by the river and in the south by a low range of hills. The children are dressed in the sturdy clothes that youngsters wore in the 1950s and, as they did in those days, they carry their school bags on their backs. Looking in one direction I see the farms where their mums and dads work and where they themselves live and play. Turning in the opposite direction I see the local primary school. It is a small, single-teacher school standing alone in the countryside, built to educate the children of the parish; a parish with only the church and the school as the social centres of its life. I see the children on their way home from a day spent learning the basic rules of spelling, grammar and sums. Having filled their heads with the no-frills education of the day, they are heading back to their no-frills homes in farm cottages or farm houses.

Home and school form the two points in the world of these children and every day, apart from school holidays, they meander to and fro between these two hubs. As they travel along they never form an orderly group. Sometimes one or two race ahead and jump on the fence wires along the road sides. Some are chatting to each other, no doubt relating stories of homework, playtime and school. Further back, there is a straggler with his school bag slipping further and further down his back, weary from the effort of a day's learning.

Suddenly there is a commotion. One small boy, with straw-coloured hair that may have been brushed at one point in the day but is now very unkempt, has picked up a large stone at the road side and is creeping up to one of the girls who is unaware he is behind her. Quietly he tries to slip the heavy stone into her school bag. His practical joke is about to be achieved when another of the small gang alerts the intended victim. With his prank foiled, the scruffy little boy moves away from the rest of the group. He seems to be dreaming, dreaming no doubt of other mischievous tricks to play. . . .

I was thinking that this was a rather good trick to play on Mary. If Cathie had not told her, then Mary would have gone home complaining about how heavy her school bag was and, even if I had not been there to see it, her mum would have opened the bag and found this big stone. I would have liked to have been there when that happened, but Cathie spoiled it.

What can I do now? I do not fancy jumping on the fence. I did that yesterday and Dad did not seem to appreciate my stories of how bouncy the wires could be. He said something about loose fence wires letting his sheep out onto the road and I would have to catch them if they escaped. I know it is not much fun to chase sheep as they seem to be particularly stupid animals and never do what you would like them to do.

I could go and check in the hedge to see if the blackbird is still sitting on her nest with four eggs in it, but Mum warned me to leave the nest alone so that the little birds can hatch out. Mostly I do what Mum says.

I could just go away and think, because when I close the rest of the world off I can just think my very own thoughts. Mrs Armstrong, my teacher, is always giving me a row for doing this. She says I am daydreaming and I am not paying attention. Teachers seem to know a great deal but they do not know about thinking. Often I am thinking about the tractors on my Dad's farm, or I am thinking about whether Mrs Armstrong will realise I have not finished doing my sums or spelling. Sometimes I am thinking about what games I will play when I go home tonight or what ploys I will get up to during school playtime tomorrow.

Just right now I am thinking I see an old man. He seems to be looking at me from his armchair, seated by the window in his little house. His face is wrinkly like old people's faces seem to be. His hair is sort of grey but it looks as if it was once straw coloured. It is rather untidy hair and I wonder if his Dad used to comb his hair when he was small like my Dad does to mine every day before I go to school.

If I listen, I think I can hear the old man's voice and he is saying, 'Remind me of the games and fun I used to have. Tell me the stories of growing up in the countryside fifty years ago, where men worked on farms and where youngsters played around farm buildings and local countryside.'

I think I might just do that.

Our Secret Hideout

THERE was no doubt it had a commanding view. Several hundred feet below us at the foot of the hill lay Dad's farm. We could see exactly what was going on. My two brothers, John and Willie, and I could see the farm house where we lived. We could even see the washing blowing on the clothes line. John reckoned this was good because Mum could secretly send messages to us by hanging out the washing in a certain way. He had seen this in a comic he had read and he claimed it had worked.

Beyond the farm, the view was dominated by the River Tay. At this point it is tidal, constantly moving from being a full, fat, mile-wide river at high tide, to a patchwork of sand and mud banks at the other point of the moon's pull. From our vantage point, we could also see across the river to the Sidlaw Hills and the flat Carse of Gowrie land where, on Sundays, we could often watch men parachute jumping from a big balloon tethered at the airfield. Dad called this a barrage balloon and said the soldiers were practising, just in case there was another war.

Back on our own side of the river, we could monitor the

coming and going of vehicles along the quiet country road that runs parallel with the Tay. We reckoned the site we had selected as a secret hideout was ideal.

My brothers and I chose an ash tree that grew at the side of the wood. Halfway up its trunk two branches grew out horizontally and these, we decided, would form the platform of our highly secret monitoring operation.

The need for secrecy and guarding our property was obvious. As children brought up in the years following the Second World War, we listened to adults as they talked about the possibility of an enemy invading our country.

We reckoned that, as small boys, it was up to us to be ready to defend our country against this threat. We told ourselves the secret hideout was no game. Many of the men on the farm still wore khaki trousers and jackets from their days in the army or as volunteers in the Home Guard. When they stopped their work and sat down for a rest to eat their pieces of bread and jam and to pour hot tea from their Thermos flasks, they often spoke about being in the army. We listened to stories of how on one Home Guard practice night, the shepherd had managed to pull the pin out of a grenade but then let it fall at his feet instead of lobbing it away as far as he could and how his life had been saved by a quick-witted officer picking the bomb up and throwing it away. The men said that this all happened in my primary school where the Home Guard met every week to practise being soldiers instead of farm workers. When I heard this, I wondered if it would not have been better to let the grenade go off and blow up the school.

John, Willie and I listened to other stories about the sentries guarding our country and falling asleep at night after working all day at the harvest. We heard how officers would come out from the towns to instruct the local Home Guard; although we heard the men say that these people just liked bossing the local workers around.

The men pointed out to us where a barrel of fuel had been stored behind a big tree that grew at the roadside so that when the German tanks came along our country road this would be tipped into their path and set alight. Thus the invading army would be stopped in its tracks. I would have liked to see that, but it never happened and when I looked, all that was left of the booby trap was a flat concrete base.

Even if the enemy came in by plane they would meet resistance. The farm workers pointed out where telegraph poles had been strategically placed in all the flat fields by the Home Guard to prevent the enemy gliders floating quietly in out of the night sky.

By this time the men had a captive audience and they elaborated on how they used to fire at enemy bombers flying over to the big industrial towns in the West of Scotland. Just before they went back to work, one of the men looked at the river and said, 'That's where they will come in.' This left us boys believing that such a possibility really existed. That was why we needed a secret hideout, so that we would be ready for any invading force.

Neither John, Willie nor I ever actually got around to working out why any enemy would come to our particular rural part of the country, remote as it was from any strategic or economic centre.

However, we raced back to the farm to get the necessary tools and material for making the hideout. There were old wooden battens in the wood pile but they looked too heavy to carry back up the hill and we decided to pinch some much lighter spars from a broken gate instead. Then it was round to the tool shed to borrow a saw, hammer and a handful of nails. The men were working around the farm but we could not reveal our plans lest they were caught and tortured by the invading enemy and forced to reveal the whereabouts of our hideout.

Some of our enthusiasm wore off as we lugged this load of building equipment back up the track that meandered up the hill. We had read that those who had climbed Mount Everest had made several camps en route, so we had several stopping points for rest. However, we eventually got all the gear up to the selected tree and started to build our hideout. In addition to hammering in a few nails for steps up to the branches we then cut down a few smaller branches to give an unimpeded view down river. Next, the flooring was laid, though that may sound grand for the half-dozen pieces of wood that were put down and then nailed together. We soon had a bird's-eye view of our small world. Willie was the first look-out and he soon reported seeing the baker's van turning into the farm, then stopping at the farm house. Rather traitorously, I wished I had asked Mum to buy my most recent favourite food, a raisin-filled slice of cake that the baker called a 'fly cemetery'. This was rather a strange name because I never saw any dead flies when I was eating it. I was feeling hungry but John said, and it must have been true as it was also in my comics, that soldiers in the armed services often went hungry. I resolved to leave a 'fly cemetery buying' message the next time I had to be on sentry duty on the same day as the baker's van was due.

As our hideout building was carried out in the quietness of the summer, when crops were growing and harvest was still a month or so away, the men were doing odd maintenance jobs around the farm. We could see them checking out machinery, getting it ready for the busy harvest period. We could also see others painting the shed doors and roof-gutters around the steading, as this was required by the landlord of the farm.

Our first surprise sighting was seeing the farm student who had been despatched to clear out the guttering on the roof of the main part of the farm steading. Out of sight of the farm grieve he seemed to be lying back motionless on the roof pantiles. We could not see if his eyes were open, but we noted down in our spy notebook that we suspected he had fallen asleep.

That was the excitement of the secret hideout. After another day or two looking in vain for an invading army that never seemed to come over the horizon, we grew tired of all the vigilance and gradually forgot our secret.

At least we forgot about it until several months later in our Christmas holidays when we were despatched to help the cattleman feed the cows grazing the field on top of the hill. As we bumped up the farm track sitting on top of a load of turnips, we looked up at the hideout. The ash tree had shed its leaves so our secret was cruelly exposed to friend and foe alike.

Sunday School

THREE large pennies were clutched in each of our little hands. There were four of us: my little sister Gina, older brothers John and Willie, and me. Between us we had one shilling which we thought might have bought a considerable amount of chocolate or sweeties the next time the grocer's van came to the farm.

However, Mum had already allocated the money. 'There is one penny for the bus to the church, one penny for putting in the church collection plate and one penny for the bus coming back,' which, I quickly worked out, meant we were financially no better off at the end of our regular Sunday morning trip than we were before it. Mum assured us we would be better children after the minister spoke to us at Sunday school, but I did not see how that could be.

We really were well behaved as we waited for the bus. This was partly because the stern warnings from Mum about looking after our good Sunday clothes were still ringing in our ears and partly because where we stood to get the bus was still very much in view from the kitchen window.

The bus rattled to a stop and the door was opened by the conductress, who seemed to resent small people boarding her bus as it interrupted her quiet peaceful Sunday morning run in the country. She did, however, come back to where we were sitting in the bus and by turning a handle on her little ticket machine she soon produced tickets in exchange for our proffered pennies. We then played at sliding back and forth along the wooden-sparred seats. The spars were quite slippy from the many hundreds of bottoms which had sat on them and occupied our minds until the conductress pressed the bell and shouted, 'Flisk Church.'

Along with other children heading for the Sunday school, we wandered down the path to the church. We could see the minister coming out of his house, still adjusting his collar which he always wore back to front. He lived next to the church and he was already at the door to meet us when we walked across the churchyard. My older brothers tried to scare me with stories of dead people and skeletons lying under the gravestones all around the church. If that was not bad enough, they then said that some of the bodies had not been properly buried and sometimes you could see a bony arm or leg sticking out of the ground. I cannot tell you if that was true or not because I never ever looked left or right as I raced from the cemetery gate to the church door.

We listened to the minister telling us about the Ten Commandments, the twelve disciples and, at Christmas time, a story about Mary and Joseph going to Bethlehem to have the baby Jesus in a cow manger. Dad had cows but we kept them in courts, not mangers, and I thought I might ask Mum if any of us had been born in a cattle court.

We sang hymns. Having been taught singing at the ordinary school, we mostly sang together but Mrs Blair, who played the church organ and sang at the same time, could hold a note much longer than we could. Often we were singing the next line before she had finished the last one. That was good as the minister looked cross when she did this because he wanted everyone to finish singing at the same time.

Sometimes, rather than singing, I preferred to look at the particles of dust dancing in the rays of sunlight that pierced through the windows. The church had stained glass windows so the sunlight came in different colours and sometimes when the sun shone this meant that the minister's face appeared to have blue and red and yellow stripes, which was very funny.

This was all before dropping my penny in the large brass plate, where it made a fine ring, before racing back up to catch the bus for the return journey. One of my friends made sure his penny made a big noise. None of the adults realised that he had only made a noise with it. After making the noise he just held on to the coin. Later, I saw him slyly sticking it back in his pocket.

Sunday school was not too bad. If we went every Sunday, we were allowed to go on the Sunday school trip in the summer where there were races and food and we could also go to the

Christmas party where there were games, food and a present.

There was one time when Dad came home from church and he was very angry. As we all sat around the dinner table he said someone – and this someone had been at Sunday school – had been kicking his shoes against the pew in front and now the wooden back of the seat was all marked with black shoe-polish type marks. He said if he ever caught the person who did this then he would smack him.

I kept my feet with my finely polished shoes well under the table in case I became a suspect.

Flour and Flesh do not Mix

BY the time my primary school moved on to learning four-letter words I already knew one and that was 'pain'. Pain happened when I fell and skinned my knee. More pain happened whenever my brother held me in a headlock and then for good measure twisted my arm up my back. I am not going to tell you that I had been pestering him for some considerable time before he took his painful revenge.

But the realest, sorest pain I ever felt was an accident. Along with both my brothers I had been playing down at the river. The main attraction was watching the men fishing for salmon. They would go out in a small boat, gradually letting their nets fall from the boat as they rowed around in a small circle before coming back to shore, where they pulled in the net. As small boys we did not have nets but we had made ourselves fishing lines which we then threw as far as we could into the water. The lines went quite far as we had tied a lump of lead to the end. The fishermen had given us a flat fish called a flounder which they did not want and which, they said, we could use as bait. So we cut up this flat fish with its silvery back and white tummy and put small pieces of it on the hooks at the ends of our lines.

Now it was not long before I realised that being a fisherman requires patience. John had some of this so he sat down and waited to see if any fish would bite. Willie just had a little patience and while, to begin with, he sat down beside John, he soon wandered off, leaving his older brother to watch both lines. I was bored with fishing and, having tied my line to a stone, I was already exploring a nearby dump. This contained things that had been thrown away as broken or worn out from both the farm and the farm cottages. I could see an old bedstead sticking up. There were also a lot of ashes as the cottage rubbish dumps were taken down to this area.

I must tell you that you had to be careful when exploring dumps because they were favourite places for rats. I could see their ratty tracks and was glad I had my wellies on so that these scurrying creatures could not run up my bare legs. Beyond the bedstead was a heap of old potatoes that were no good for market so Dad had brought them down to this dump by the riverside. There was also a heap of straw which I remembered one of the farm men had carted down earlier in the week. He had set light to it and, even though it was two days later, some of the straw was still smouldering away with little puffs of smoke coming out of the ashes. As I trudged through it I could still feel the warmth from the burnt straw. There were no flames, so as far as I knew the fire was out. Then I felt this pain, this big, big pain as some of the burning straw came over the top of my wellies and down my leg.

'Get some flour to cool it down,' I heard the fisherman who was looming over me shout. The team of men who had been fishing only a minute or two earlier were now all peering down at my melted wellie. I looked at where they were looking and then looked away as a burned leg is very sore but not very pretty. I did not know at the time but Mum said later that melted rubber, flour and burnt skin is not a good mix. She said this after I had been given a piggy-back home by one of the men and taken up to my bed. The doctor came and looked at my leg and agreed that flour may have been the right thing to use for making cakes but it was not a good idea for curing burned legs. I had to stay in bed for a week. Dad made me a wire cage to keep the weight of the heavy blankets off my leg. Normally that would have been fun to play in but if you have a sore leg then hitting it against a wire cage when you are asleep is not fun.

John came in and said he had caught a big fish on his fishing line. Thinking he had caught a salmon, I asked how big the fish was and he held his hands out. Perhaps they were not fully out-stretched but it did seem that he had caught a pretty big fish. He left with a smile on his face and it was some time later that I found out there had been no salmon.

He had caught a fish and it was quite long, but then eels can be quite lengthy.

My 'Going Away' Holiday

IT was a long time before I knew what a 'going away' holiday was. I knew about holidays from school. These were when my pals and I raced about the farm playing various games and generally getting in the way of the men trying to do their work. But a 'packing a suitcase and going away in the car' holiday was a strange thing to think about. Both my older brothers had been on this type of holiday and they spoke about the sandy beach and the big play gardens when they came back from Scarborough. Now, I knew about sandy beaches as we sometimes went to St Andrews, so I knew it was good fun to dig tunnels and build castles in the sand. I also knew from my visits to St Andrews that the sea was either cold or very cold and that after jumping in the waves for a few minutes all your skin had little bumps on it. 'Goose pimples' my Mum called them as she wrapped our little white bodies up in a big, dry towel and gave us a biscuit to eat. This was called a 'shivery bite'. True enough, without even trying to eat, our teeth would chitter through the biscuit as we recovered from our exposure to the chilly North Sea.

I had not been on a holiday where you stayed in a place called a 'Bed and Breakfast' before and where there were things to do especially for people on holiday. I had missed the family trip to Scarborough because at the last minute the doctor said I had measles and so Granny was called upon to look after me as the rest of the family drove off. It was not too bad after they had gone, even if I was left with no one to fight with. The only bad bit came at night time when Granny always asked me if I had washed my face before going to bed. She never did believe me when I said yes. My Granny had powerful strong hands and soon a slightly grubby neck was being scrubbed quite fiercely. Much as I tried, there was no wriggling away from the face-cleaning performance.

A whole year passed and there was some excitement because the family was going to Ayr for yet another holiday. I could not understand it but it seemed that people went on holiday every year. My older brothers and I knew something was going on when Dad got the suitcase down from the top of the wardrobe. It was explained that we three boys had to share this one case for our clothes. We ran through to little sister Gina's room and, sure enough, she had a suitcase for herself. Admittedly it was much smaller but I still think she was spoiled. As it was, the clothes we three boys decided to take could not even fill our case, but that was not the point.

I had marked the day we were going on holiday on the calendar in the kitchen and soon it was only six days before we would tie our cases to the roof of the car and head for this place called 'Ayr'.

And that was when I stepped into a heap of burning straw and burned my leg. Mum asked about me going on holiday and I heard the doctor, whom I had previously liked, say, 'I don't think so.' I can tell you now that it took a great deal of little boy whining and wheedling before Mum and Dad decided to take me. I was pretty pleased with myself by the time the heavily laden car with the whole family aboard left the farm. My leg was still bandaged up so I was allowed to sit in the front of the car and that was better. But what was not good was that when we got there I was not allowed near the sea or even the sand.

There were also some arguments between my brothers. Mum had decided that my burned leg should be rested and she had tied an old pushchair on top of the luggage on top of the car. She had also decided that John and Willie should take turns in pushing their little brother around in this chair and that was where the arguments started. Not as I would have thought, with them both wanting to do this; quite the opposite in fact, which I thought was not very encouraging for a little boy with a bad leg waiting to be propelled along the beach front at Ayr.

It was not long before I was none too sure about bed and breakfast places. My brothers and I used to rush from room to room through our house but this place we were staying in did not seem to support these games of chasing, catching and fighting. Another thing struck me as I listened to the other grown-up people in the bed and breakfast. They said they did not like a great deal of noise, so Mum warned us to be quiet and for most of the time we were.

However, I was happy, because when I went back home to the farm I could tell my friends at school that I had been on a 'going away' holiday, even if I had gone with just one good leg.

Food, Glorious Food

IT was really all about timing. Get it wrong and you could be marched back to bed. Get it right and a veritable feast awaited you.

For hungry school children, the first signs became evident early in the day. The table in the dining room had been set and we could count that, even after subtracting Dad and Mum's places at either end of the table, there was room for another six people and my brothers and I knew we were not in that number.

A quick scurry through to the kitchen confirmed we were going to have visitors. Mum was busy putting pots and pans into the oven and there was evidence of cooking all around.

The clinching factor came at our normal tea time of five o'clock. We had our tea and then either Mum or Dad would say, 'We want you off to bed early tonight.' That confirmed it and so we went through the routine of being scrubbed clean and then marched upstairs well before our normal bed time.

This was where the importance of timing came in. It was no good appearing downstairs as soon as we heard the visitors' cars crunch the gravel outside the house. We listened carefully as the door bell rang and the visitors came in. Some voices we recognised. Others we did not. Sometimes we stuck our heads through the banisters in an attempt to see the visitors coming in. On one occasion, this curiosity was almost the cause of a major disaster as little sister Gina managed to get her head through the banisters but could not get it back out again. There was a danger that if we left her there she would make a noise and our great plans for later would be irreparably damaged, so it was quite clever of John to push the rest of her body through between the two posts and onto the narrow ledge overlooking the hall, then pull her back over the top.

This diversion from the main target of the night was unfortunate but we were soon back on course as the food was carried through from the kitchen. Next was the worst part of waiting. We discussed what the visitors were eating and sometimes we tried to guess by the smells that wafted up into our bedroom; but that was a pretty useless and frustrating exercise. Quietness was paramount. We did not want an irate parent coming upstairs to ensure the brood was sound asleep.

After what seemed ages, we heard plates being taken back to the kitchen followed by the rattle of the tea trolley going in the opposite direction. We looked at each other and whispered, 'not long now.' Cigarette smoke curled up through a house that normally never experienced such pollution. Sometimes, we could smell pipe smoke or even on odd occasions, the rich smell of cigars.

32

That was when we decided it was safe to go downstairs. Usually we would send Gina down first. If there were still adults around, then she always seemed to be guaranteed to escape any wrathful blast.

We boys scuttled down behind and soon we were in the kitchen where among the empty plates were the remains of the meal. Having had our tea, it was not really hunger that drove us on such foraging expeditions. But the sight of a large bowl of Mum's trifle or a dish of wobbly jelly with more than half of it still uneaten was mouth watering.

Just as we children could never understand the magic of the tooth fairy finding a broken tooth under our pillows and then replacing it with a silver sixpence, and just as this magic person called Santa Claus came and gave us presents every year, other miracles happened. I am sure Mum and Dad were often astonished to find all the leftover food cleaned up. Well, perhaps not all of it. The puddings were the first target, as we were not so keen on eating cold boiled potatoes or Brussels sprouts or peas or anything else that we normally considered as food.

We staggered upstairs before the adults emerged from the dining room and I cannot recall much more about these evenings except for when Mr and Mrs X were visitors. He was generally very noisy by the time he left and we listened as his wife tried to persuade him it was time to go home. It was strange that he did not want to go as he had had his supper.

Then there was always once every year when nobody seemed

to come very early to visit and they all made a noise right through the night when we were trying to sleep. Mum called it Hogmanay and we knew it was coming around because everything in the house was cleaned and tidied 'for the New Year' Mum said, when we asked.

But I never saw much difference between a dull December day and an equally dull January one. Adults have strange customs.

The Trouble with Travel

As soon as we knew we were going out in the car, the arguments started. 'Bags me the side seat,' one brother shouted.

This was followed quickly by my other brother coming in with, 'Bags me the other side seat.' That was the start. It then became worse.

'You had the side seat last time.'

'No I didn't.'

'Oh yes you did.' The clever bit was not to stand and argue but to make a quick dash to the back seat of the car and sit down next to the door, locking it immediately to repel invaders. My older brother John called this a 'bums on seats' policy which caused him to get a row from Mum but it seemed to work. The two brothers left behind by this sudden action would then dash to the other side and physical hostilities would break out as they jostled to sit in the remaining side seat.

The next link in this happy family chain of events was a bellow from Mum or Dad, saying that if we did not behave, then none of us would go. That had only the superficial effect of quelling the immediate fighting which was soon replaced by more subtle aggression. I can tell you that a sneaky poke in the ribs or a kick on the legs could sometimes disturb one of the incumbents of the coveted seat by the window or at least trigger off a row from Dad following any retaliation.

And what was all this arguing about? If you are still under ten years old it is important to see beyond your own backyard. The seat by the window ensured that you saw everything that was going on when we went on our family travels. Most people know there are only two side seats in the back of the car and there were three brothers. Apart from this arithmetic, the middle seat was higher than the others and was uncomfortable. If I sat there as the little old car swung round the corners, I would fall against one brother or the other. Thus the risk of escalating a bout of petty warfare was high.

Meanwhile our little sister, Gina, sat in the middle in the front, wedged between Dad who was driving and Mum who had a full-time occupation as peacemaker.

The good part about sitting in the middle in the back seat was that you could give your little sister a sneaky nip in her back while quickly assuming an air of complete innocence when the 'little girl' squeals came out.

As we drove along Dad would regale us with threats of what would happen if we did not behave and he also told us about when his Mum and Dad took his family of eight brothers and sisters out for a Sunday afternoon run. He said that when the family car reached a hill the bigger boys had to get out and walk so that the old car could puff its way to the top of the incline.

On our trips, we gradually settled down and travelling games were played so that Mum did not have to keep answering 'Are we there yet?' These were fairly straightforward games, such as looking for different colours or cars or playing 'I spy' which always started quite well but ended up with someone claiming they saw something that none of the rest of us did. Dad would never turn the car back to prove whether the 'spied' object really had existed.

By this time the car had warmed up and he was driving quite fast so that the car was swinging along the narrow roads. This was the cue for a small voice to say, 'I don't feel well. I think I am going to be sick.'

This prediction caused several reactions. Mum reached for the towel which she always carried. Dad slammed on the brakes so that the child about to vomit could get out of the car before any accident happened. The healthy children suddenly gave the ailing one far more room than they had only seconds before.

Sometimes, the prediction was correct and a little pool of lunch or tea was left by the roadside. The rest of us looked out of the window to see the performance, but that did not make us feel any better. As a precaution, the rather pale and wan child would then get one of the favoured side seats by the window just in case they might put on a repeat performance.

I wondered about taking this sickness option in order to get the side seat, but really, sitting in the middle was no great problem.

Almost an Early Bath

A T first I thought I had escaped. Along with my brothers I
had been watching the sheep on the farm being put
through the dipper. This involved the farm men catching them
and then pushing them backwards into this deep bath which was
not just full of cold water but was also coloured a bright, bright
yellow with a fluid that Dad had poured out of a tin. He told us
that this magic potion, with its very noticeable skull and cross-
bones on the side of the tin and a word that so far had not come
up in my school spelling but which my brothers said was
'poison', would kill all the little insects that lived on the skin of
the sheep.

The shepherd, in a hole specially dug out in the ground right
beside the dipper, caught the sheep and expertly pushed their
heads under the water, at the same time turning them around.
After a few seconds he released the sheep and each one made a
surging swim to dry land at the other end of the bath. Quickly
climbing the concrete steps in the bath the sheep made its exit,
shaking its fleece vigorously as it found itself once again on dry
land.

My brothers and I were always fascinated by this performance. Apart from any other reason it was one of the few occasions that we country children saw the local policeman. The police had to attend sheep dippings to ensure they were properly carried out and, as the man in blue uniform told us wide-eyed children, they helped prevent the spread of disease. But it never appeared to us that the policeman was very interested. Preventing the spread of disease seemed quite a quiet occupation for a policeman. He just sat in his car smoking his cigarettes while watching the men wrestle with the sheep before despatching them into the dipper. The policeman did emerge from his vehicle but, as my brother John pointed out to me, it was nearly lunchtime by then and back at the house when we sat down to eat an extra place had been set.

The problem for me, and indeed for John and Willie, was that from our observation point in one corner of the sheep pens we could see the men sometimes losing their footing as a particularly awkward sheep took an extreme dislike to its impending bath. I had a degree of sympathy with that view as bathing did not come high on my own agenda. But sometimes in dealing with these stubborn animals the men would slip and fall, landing in among the sheep's dung. This caused great hilarity and that prompted the men to shout that they would catch us and throw us in the dipper after they were finished with the sheep.

That is why I came to be hanging upside down over the bath. Below I could see the cold and by now dirty water. I did not know whether to struggle as I might by accident cause the foreman to lose the vice-like grip that he had on my ankles. After what seemed like several hours of imagining just how deep and dirty the bath would be and wondering if I would be protected forever from having insects living on me, I was released. Much, I may say, to the disappointment of the rest of the farm workforce.

Sheep were part and parcel of the farm and, in the early springtime, we often came down the stairs in the mornings to find a lamb curled up in a piece of sacking inside a cane basket which was placed in front of an open door of the cooker. Outside, the day could be sleety, wet and cold and being born in such conditions, with possibly a first-time mum, was not such a great idea. So Dad would bring frozen little lambs into the house to thaw out. We were warned not to touch or pet them as our human smells would put the mother off when the lamb was returned. The idea that we small boys did smell a bit was a discussion point between us brothers for a short time, but we dismissed it as adult talk with absolutely no foundation.

As life returned to the little lambs, they would sometimes get up out of their basket and wander around the kitchen simultaneously bleating and piddling. This was a signal for Mum to insist the little lamb was returned immediately to its mother outside. Dad, accompanied by his own brood who wanted to see the action, would then pick the little animal up under his arm and go out to the lambing shed.

Carefully he would reintroduce the lamb to the mother ewe that had been held in a pen made of straw bales. We were told firstly to keep out of sight and secondly to keep quiet. I do not think we managed either as we wanted to see the family reunion but the double caution at least kept us from messing about and fighting to the same extent as normal.

Sometimes, if a baby lamb had died, the shepherd would skin it and then tie the skin onto another lamb whose mother had produced triplets and could not look after all three. Although it was easy for me to see where the old skin was tied onto the lamb, the new mother did not seem to notice and she looked after her new offspring as if it were her own.

A month or so later we were back as a ready audience after the lambing was completed and the whole enlarged flock of ewes and lambs was brought back into the sheep pens. There was always a great deal of bleating and that was before the lambs knew they were going to have their tails cut off. Dad said this was necessary as it stopped them having a dirty bottom. I suppose our tails had been cut off a long time ago to prevent something similar happening. We saw the shepherd sharpening the knife on a stone on which he spat before pulling the blade back and forward. 'Did spittle sharpen knives?' I wondered, but there was no one prepared to answer what I thought was a fairly straightforward question.

A similar lack of response met my next question. It was soon obvious that about half of the lambs were not just having their tails cut off, but having another part of their anatomy between their legs opened up, which the shepherd then squeezed until two grey-coloured pieces of meat appeared from the open wound. He then bit them with his teeth and with a quick pull and twist of his head, these same grey stone lumps lay in a bucket beside him.

'What are all these for?' I wondered, only to hear a mono-syllabic response. 'Soup,' he muttered.

When questioned by me later, Mum said she didn't know anything about this part of the performance, or at least she was not saying.

42

Coronation Day

AFTER we had all trooped into our little primary school, Mrs Armstrong, the teacher, said she had an important announcement to make. I looked across at David as many of the teacher's important announcements seemed to refer to one or other of us, but it was obvious from the shake of his head that neither of us felt we were guilty on this occasion.

'The King is dead,' she said. I do not think anyone at our school had ever met him but it seemed to be important. The King ran the country after all and I suppose decided important things such as how many holidays we should have from school and possibly even what price my Dad's potatoes should be. I knew the King did not decide what the weather was going to be. Somebody else decided that and that person was not Dad's best friend when the weather was bad.

I thought, 'we will need a new King' but before I could ask about this, Mrs Armstrong said there would be a Queen this time.

That was before one day, which would normally have been a school day, when Dad packed the whole family up and we went along to Granny's. We were to see the coronation of the new Queen on a television set and none of us, except possibly Dad, had ever seen such a contraption before.

I had heard the men talking about television one day as I watched them working in the field. I told them my Granny had a television set and I was going along to see it. One of them asked if it was an electrical television set but I did not know the answer to that question. At this point another of the tractormen said he had heard that gas-powered television gave better pictures and I was thinking about this when the grieve, who was working at the end of the sugar-beet thinning line, took his pipe out of his mouth and said the best televisions were those that were powered by paraffin. I knew that this fuel made the lights glow and it could be used for heating cookers, but I did not know about it being able to make moving pictures so I said nothing.

I did ask Mum when I went back for my lunch and she laughed and told me she wished the men were as good at working as they were at telling stories. She told me a story of her own about the young boy who had just started work on the farm when the older men asked him to go round to the workshop for a tin of tartan paint. She laughed, but I thought that would be really valuable, especially if it came in different tartans.

Granny's television was in the corner of the room and it seemed as if she had invited everyone in the street to watch it. Once you had a little space in the room you were jammed in

44

and it needed a pretty good plan even to get out to the toilet. We sat for hours and hours watching the black and white pictures of the new Queen in her carriage and all the crowds waving in the wet weather. Then there was singing and I saw the crown being placed on her head. My brothers and I went out to play after that as we had been sitting for hours and hours and hours. Not long after that Dad called us to take us back home.

But Coronation day was not finished as there were races and games for all the people who lived in the area. All the children at the school received a mug with the Queen's picture on one side of it and a big silver coin in a special box. But then we were told we could not spend the coin in the shops or even in the vans that came around to our farms because it was a special coin. Having money you cannot spend on sweets did not seem a good idea to me.

I did hold onto it just in case it would be valuable, but I really did not think it would because everyone I knew at school had one.

After the sports we went home, but still Coronation day was not finished as Mum got us all tidied up for the barn dance that was to be held that night in a shed on Jim's dad's farm. I was already quite tired and in spite of all the music and dancing going on I soon fell asleep on the straw bales. I missed the bonfire that was set alight on the top of the hill when it was dark.

But I did dream about there being loads more coronations, as they seemed to be lots of fun.

Chickens and Christmas

THEY lay on the kitchen table, their bodies naked and
white, with just a feather here and there. Their scrawny
necks and red-combed heads hung over the side of the table
with just the occasional drop of blood falling onto the old newspaper that covered the linoleum floor.

The hens were laid out lifeless on the table waiting for the
visit of Aunt Beth. I knew that Aunt Beth had gone to college to
study important things such as how to make butter and cheese.
She had also been taught about keeping hens and my older
brothers, John and Willie, told me Aunt Beth even knew how
to kill hens when they stopped laying eggs. What they did not
say was that she could then prepare these dead hens for cooking
and for me that was really good news as it meant chicken for
Sunday lunch.

Although the hens may not have appreciated the fact, it
meant that it was a good time of year, because the killing of the
hens always took place a week before Christmas.

Two days before the kitchen table had been covered with all
the dead hens, I had been curled up in a trough in one of the

small cattle sheds. The trough was a safe place and a good observation point. Ropes had been slung over the wooden rafters of the shed. Then the hens squawking and clucking their last were dragged out of a wooden crate. Dad grabbed the birds by their legs and then with a quick pull and twist of his hands broke their necks. As I watched wide eyed, the now dead bird continued to flap and writhe about. Once one escaped and fluttered across the straw and I heard Dad say something about 'It's just nerves,' but it all seemed a bit spooky to me. As quickly as possible the bird was hung up by its legs on the ropes and the plucking commenced, as Dad said it was much easier to remove the feathers when the blood in the hen was still warm.

Only after I was convinced that the hen was definitely dead did I venture out of the trough where I had been hiding. I helped, especially with plucking the breast and back feathers as these were the easy parts. I saw how the men at the plucking grasped handfuls of feathers and quickly pulled them against the way they lay on the body. Soon stretches of white hen skin appeared. Sometimes, if the plucker was careless, the skin was torn. Dad would 'tut tut' if that happened with one of the men, but if I tore the skin when practising my plucking it usually meant being sent back to observe proceedings from the cattle trough. I tried to pull out the wing feathers but they were always difficult and sometimes, if it was a tough old cockerel that was being plucked, Dad would have a pair of pliers to pull the very biggest of the feathers.

I should have said that the whole process had started the previous weekend, when Dad had gone round the various henhouses and picked out those hens that had given up laying eggs. I noticed that he normally chose those birds whose combs were no longer bright red, whose feathers were coming out and who clucked obstinately when he picked them up.

The reduction of the number of hens Dad kept was welcome, as the first job my brothers and I had when we came home from school was to feed the hens and collect the eggs. Mostly this was no problem, but sometimes if an old hen was sitting on the nest she would make an angry cluck and even try to peck the egg collector. It was possible to try and just lift her gently and then put your hand into the nest and pull the eggs out, but Mrs Hen continued to let you know she was not too happy. After we had collected the eggs from the nestboxes we would look around the rest of the henhouse as some of the hens seemed to lay their eggs anywhere. Mum said they were like little children just leaving their toys all around the room, but I did not understand what she meant.

Once when I was collecting eggs I found out about gravity and centrifugal force, but really it was just a bit of fun that my brothers and I got up to. After we had gathered all the eggs into the basket we would take them back to the house. On the journey, John started to swing the basket. First it was just back and forward and then, without warning, he swung the basket right around his head. Seeing the eggs upside down in the basket and yet not falling out was fun and I wondered if I could do the same. John was not keen that I do the experiment with a full basket and so we emptied most of the eggs onto the ground. With only a few left, he let me try to swing the basket around my head. As the eggs fell about me and then spattered on the ground, he told me that I needed more speed in swinging the bucket. Looking at the damage, it had been a good move to take most of the eggs out of the basket. I also remembered that he had looked all around before he did his little trick just in case some of the adults found out what he was about to do.

When Aunt Beth did arrive, she was carrying a bundle of tools in a little canvas bag and when she opened this up I saw the big sharp knives that she was going to use. I also saw the largest darning needle I had ever seen. To begin with I did not see just how sharp it was, as she kept a cork on the end of it.

My brothers and I were allocated minor jobs around the table, such as ensuring there was string in the big needle she used to sewed up the carcase. One job we did not like was taking the sloppy bucket with the hen guts out to the cattle courts where we had to lift a wedge of straw bedding and then tip the unwanted contents out before covering them up. We had seen the strings of intestines being pulled out from a hole Aunt Beth made in the hen's bottom. We had also seen the giblets and neck being laid to one side for making soup. Sometimes Aunt Beth also showed us the egg-laying parts of the hen with a string of partially formed eggs inside a tube. My brothers and I talked about all these things as we took the full bucket away for burial.

The trussed-up birds were quickly transferred to the pantry where they were laid in rows on the stone shelves.

Normally this room had rows of apples laid out along the top shelves and then there was a whole shelf with bottles of pears and plums in Kilner jars and different kinds of jam that Mum had made in the summer. In the corner was a big glass-lined chest with one side full of oatmeal for the porridge we had every morning. The other half was filled with flour for Mum's baking which we were warned not to go near – although I never understood why grubby small boys could not play with their tractors in this fine, white powder. But now it seemed as if the whole pantry was full of dead hens.

At this point Dad and Mum started putting tickets with names under the birds. Some were Christmas presents for the farm workers. Smaller ones were laid aside for houses where there was only a man and his wife, larger birds were kept for those with families. In the coming days, we would be allowed to take the hens on our piler, or barrow, along with other bits and pieces such as shortbread or black bun that formed the Christmas parcel for the workforce.

Other hens were destined for Dad's business contacts, with favoured salesmen who always seemed to visit the farm in the week before Christmas being top of the list. For a reason that I never did work out, the banker always received a particularly chubby-breasted bird. The minister was also on the list, but I recall the size of the hen seemed to relate to Dad's latest opinion on the workings of the Kirk Session or even just the quality of recent sermons.

By this time, the shelves were getting bare and we worried in case Mum had miscounted. Imagine, we thought, if everyone else had a hen for Christmas and we did not.

It never happened, of course, but it was a worry until we saw the cooked white meat on our plate. Possibly because we only had it on rare occasions – chicken or old hen always meant clean, clean plates.

False Alarm

'I'M killed! I'm killed!' came the screams from my little sister, Gina. This was rather strange, because whenever people were killed in my comics, they never announced the fact. All that generally happened as the grenade blew them up or the machine gun bullets ripped into their bodies, was a balloon coming out of their mouths saying 'Aaaarrgh.'

I also thought that if that was the case and she had been killed, it would be a pity, because despite the fact she was a girl, we had often enjoyed playing together. She did have failings, though. For instance, there was no good fighting with her because she quickly ran to Mum before any hefty blows could be dealt.

However, when Willie and I looked back from our perch just behind the tractor driver's seat, we could see our little sister lying quite still in the brown earth with the tyre marks of the fertiliser spreader neatly across her middle. I thought 'she will get a row from Mum for making a mess of her coat', but did not mention this to the driver who had brought his tractor to a sudden stop while he jumped off and ran back to tend to the self-proclaimed deceased child.

No doubt he was concerned that he would be in trouble for

allowing Gina to ride on the machine as it bumped its way up and down the field sowing fertiliser for the planned crop of sugar beet. The machine was safe when it was full of the grey granules and we knew that it was only when it emptied there was a danger. Then you could get caught up in the rotating spiked roller that churned around just above the holes through which the granules fell onto the ground. The roller was there to break down any lumps in the fertiliser. It was not intended to mince up small sisters.

However, this was not the reason for the incident, as it appeared that Gina was sitting on the top of the spreader when it went over a bump. She bounced off in front of the wheel and it rolled over her.

I wondered why, when it had obviously run over her middle, the tractor driver asked if she could wiggle her toes. But wiggle them she did and soon, far from being dead, she was sitting up in the soft earth as if nothing had happened. She must have been well as she steadfastly refused to let her big brothers see her bare tummy to check if the wheel tread marks had gone right through her clothes. This was a pity because in the comics when people were run over, they were often squashed flat and you could see the wheel marks.

Not much later my, by now far from dead, sister was eating her lunch and all the while telling Mum and Dad about her accident.

I kept quiet but I did wonder why she never got a row after getting her coat in such a muddy mess.

A Floating Experiment

I recall the teacher telling my primary class that we should experiment in order to find out which things floated in water and which sank to the bottom. I tested it in the bath that night and some things such as a stone that I had in my pocket before bath time definitely did not float. I was in a bigger quandary with the sponge. It was a sort of 'in between' type of thing, not making up its mind whether to sink gradually down in the 'little boy murky' bath water, or to try and survive on the surface. My brothers were called in but they were no help in solving this major conundrum. However, a few days later, my brothers and I decided to test the floatability of a large wooden box which we had found down by the side of the River Tay.

It was a box used by the commercial salmon fishing company that operated during the summer months. Squads of men would come and live in the small stone bothies that were scattered along the river banks. We would watch these men cast their nets into the water and then slowly and laboriously pull them in. We watched in excitement as the pouch of the net came close to the shore. When we could see some thrashing about in the water that meant there were fish in the net.

I was somewhat mystified when the fishermen talked about the catch. Long before we smaller people could see anything, they would say something that sounded like 'We've got two fish and a trout.' Now, if my picture book on fishes was correct, then trout were fish just as there were other fish such as herring and haddock. Not that we saw any herring or haddock in the fishermen's nets. Thankfully the man in charge of the netting squad explained that they considered salmon as the only real fish, the others were all called by their own names. Sometimes adults make things very difficult for young people I thought, but I said nothing.

I said nothing, either, when they brought in a dead salmon with a big bite out of its body. The men pointed out into the water and showed me the bobbing head of a seal. I did not see its face very well but it might have been smiling a big wide smile because it had just had lunch. On our next visit a week or two later, my brothers and I came across a dead seal with its tail hacked off. John told me that whoever had killed the seal had also received a reward of ten shillings from the fishing company man.

I was telling you about the net coming in, and as it came into the shore, I saw two salmon and the smaller body of a sea trout. One member of the team with a wooden club in his hand went into the water and, with a quick blow to the heads of the fish, quickly despatched all three.

Like big bars of silver, the dead fish were laid inside wooden boxes ready to be taken away by the company boat. Mum and Dad told me later that they went away to markets in faraway towns where rich people lived and where they ate salmon. Although we were not rich, I can tell you that once a year we received a salmon from the company man because Dad had helped the men get their fishing equipment down to the bothy from the farm and Mum would help when they ordered groceries from the travelling vans. Within a few days of getting the big fish in its woven basket, visitors would be invited to lunch and Mum would curl this big fish up inside the biggest pot in the kitchen. The big fish did not take long to cook. Perhaps it knew there were a number of hungry mouths waiting for it.

Down at the shore, my brothers, sister and I wandered away from the fishermen because it seemed to take ages for them to get the next net in the water. A short distance along the shore we came across this empty box and that was when we decided to proceed further with our floating experiment.

John and Willie dragged it down the shore and then pushed it into the water. It seemed to float, but it was obvious to me that a bigger experiment was needed. The box was big enough for a passenger – a small one. We looked around and persuaded Gina that this was a grand experiment and she should be pleased, possibly even honoured, to be allowed to take part in it. She dutifully sat down in the box and we boys pushed it away from the shore. She waved and the experiment was very successful in proving that a wooden box, with a small sister in it, floats.

However, I think it was John who pointed out we had not put in place a retrieval plan, to get either the box or the little sister back. We did not know about tides but the water was definitely further down the shore than it had been when we arrived. By the time she went sailing past the fishermen, Gina was moving quite fast in mid river. The fishermen did not realise it was part of an experiment but they must have decided she might well end up down in the big city of Dundee unless they took quick action. So the next boat did not take the nets out, it went off after my sister's little boat. Although the experiment was very successful, my brothers and I decided it was not necessary to tell Mum and Dad.

I thought about our trial some time later when the teacher told my class that a cat has nine lives and I wondered how many lives little sisters have.

Decisions, Decisions

I was walking home from school thinking about making decisions. It seemed to be easy if you were an adult. The teacher made decisions on what subjects she would teach that day. She also made decisions as to when she rang the bell for playtime and although I always thought she was late in doing so, I never mentioned this to her.

My mother made decisions about what we would have for tea. I might have said she also made decisions about when we would have tea but I think Dad made the decision that tea was at five o'clock every day. Dad made other decisions. If we were up early, we could look out of our bedroom window and see Dad talking to the farm grieve. Between them, they decided what the men would be working at that day.

That left me, and there were still a great deal of decisions to be made. For instance, after tea all the children from the farm cottages would come along to the farm. Sometimes, if it was a sunny evening, they even came from the next farm and they would want to play. That was where there was a need for a definite decision. Often there was a demand for hide and seek and sometimes that could be fun, but as someone who knew every nook and cranny in all the farm buildings, I could safely hide and never be found and it was not a lot of fun to hide for hours and not be found.

One autumn, when the grain was being threshed by the mill, there was a big stack made with bunches of straw. We could climb up on this and, having seen the Olympic Games on my Granny's television, we would practise diving from the top of the stack. Neither I nor any of my pals had worked out how you could win a gold medal for diving but our attempts became more and more adventurous. To begin with we just jumped off the top and landed on some loose straw on the ground and then David showed us how to do a swallow dive landing on his tummy. I tried it but my landing was painful and I could not speak for a minute or two to tell him that. By this time, he was trying a somersault dive which looked pretty spectacular but I was not sure I could actually complete the turn, so I decided we would play another game.

We went round to the sheds where the cattle were kept in the winter. Along one side was a row of hay racks where the cattle would feed when they were kept inside. We climbed up into the rack and then onto the roof rafters where we could crawl from one side of the shed to the other. I say 'we', but by this time some of the gang had turned back saying that if we fell, the landing might be quite hard and the stop rather sudden.

It was my brother Willie who suggested the next game. He

had seen a picture of Tarzan in his comic and he said Tarzan could swing from one tree to the next in the jungle, just by using creepers that hung down from the trees. We had no creepers on the farm but we did have ropes and we soon sent Gina round to the farm tool shed to borrow some. It was always better to send her as she would get any row that might erupt over missing tools. When she returned with the ropes we threw them over the rafters and practised swinging from the hay racks right across the court. We did this for some time before there was a loud crack as one of the rafters fell down. It seemed to say, 'I have been here for one hundred years and have never had such treatment.' The remains of the gang then had a short conference and we decided to return the ropes quietly. We had made knots in the ropes for sitting on as we swung about and we were unable to untie these, but we did not think the men would notice the next time they wanted to use their ropes.

Another night we decided to take a big tyre up the hill behind the farm and then let it roll down the steep slope. Once we started, it soon gathered speed. It hit the first fence and bounced right over. It was going even faster when it hit the next fence and it bounced even higher over it. The third fence was the one at the road side. We looked to see if any cars were coming because it might have been a shock for a driver to see a big wheel bounce over the road in front of him. We never played that game again.

Most of the time, Mum did not know where we had been

playing or what we had been up to, but there were exceptions. She seemed to know right away if we had been playing near the silage pit or even the dung midden as she made us take our clothes off before we even stepped into the house. Then we were marched straight off to the bath as she said we smelled.

I hoped that when I grew up I would not have to make as many decisions as I had to do just now.

A Visit from the Queen

EVEN if you are busy discussing tractors with your best friend David, when the teacher claps her hands and says she has an important announcement, it is a good idea to stop and listen to her. With groundless optimism, I thought it might be news about an extra day's holiday or even just being released early from school that day.

However, after gaining the attention of all twenty pupils in her school, Mrs Armstrong told us that an important visitor was coming to Flisk. I thought that sometimes on the farm we had important visitors. When the vet came to help one of the cows that could not get back onto her feet or a sheep that was having trouble lambing, Dad always said that he was an important visitor. Also, although Dad did not say so, when somebody came to check the papers in the farm office, this person with the grey suit and a funny hat which bobbled about on his head when he got out of his little black Austin car was also important. My brothers and I knew of this man's importance because whenever he was there we were warned not to go into the office to play our noisy games.

So who would be important enough to come to see us at school, I wondered? There was no need of a vet as there were no animals at school other than the school goldfish that just swam round and round in its bowl. I hoped it was no one to look at the school records because that might lead to some of the less well-behaved children, which often included me, being questioned.

'The Queen is coming to Flisk,' said Mrs Armstrong, 'and we will all go out and meet her.'

'Well that is not too bad,' I thought. I had seen photos of the Queen in the newspaper my Mum and Dad read and I would recognise her because she wore a crown. David said that he would tell the Queen that his dad had got a new red tractor but I told him that was a silly thing to say because when you saw pictures of the Queen she always had people whispering in her ear and these people would already have told her that David's dad had a new tractor. But, all the same, I thought that I would stand beside David because if he started talking about tractors to the Queen I wanted to tell her that my Dad's tractors were not only bigger, they were also better.

By this time Mrs Armstrong had asked one of her favourite pupils, Cathie, to go to the cupboard where there was a box full of little flags.

'I want you to line up along the roadside when the Queen's car passes this afternoon. When she goes past we will all wave our flags.'

Somebody wondered where the Queen was going and the teacher told us, 'She is going to visit Lord Dundee.'

Well, that sorted out David and his plan to tell the Queen about tractors, I thought. Then I started to wonder why the Queen was going to visit a lord. I remembered that sometimes Mum had visitors who came to our house in the afternoon. They played cards, ate sandwiches and drank cups of tea. I suppose the Queen could be going to play cards, eat sandwiches and drink tea because that seemed something that adults did.

But I bet you she would not have sandwiches like my Mum's. For some reason that I never found out, there were special sandwiches for these card-playing visitors. They were cut into three-cornered shapes, had the crusts cut off and had special things like tomatoes or cucumbers in them.

I wondered why adults had three-cornered sandwiches when we were given big square pieces of bread. I never did discover why we had to eat our crusts because, if they were good for us, why did adults get to cut the crusty bits off? And why did we get raspberry jam or cheese and they got tomatoes, cucumbers, meat paste and other things on their sandwiches that never seemed to feature on our school pieces?

There was so much to wonder about that I almost missed the school being marched out into the playground, especially since we were told to drink our school milk before we went out to see the Queen. Even though we were a small school, there was a whole crate of milk dropped off by van and each of us got a small bottle. The milk was not too good. It must have been an old, smelly cow that it came from as the milk from my uncle's farm was sweet and fresh compared with the stale school stuff. However, it could not have been too bad as one day Ronnie found a little dead mouse in his bottle. I thought this little mouse must have just gone for a drink before the milkman put a lid on the bottle. But I noticed that Ronnie did not drink his milk for the whole of the next week.

Then, after we had drunk our milk, we were lined up along the roadside and warned not to jump on the fence wires or squeeze through onto the roadside verge. The Queen was about to come so the girls practised a little flag waving to pass the time. Some of the boys wanted to use the little flags as swords but Mrs Armstrong did not like this idea and told us so in a severe voice.

It was nothing to do with the Queen coming but I noticed that, just like other times when Mrs Armstrong used this severe voice, the rest of the boys seemed to move back quietly, magically leaving me in the front when I hadn't even moved.

The Queen did not come for a long, long time. We waved to the baker as he passed in his van and he looked slightly surprised at the reception he got, but he did not stop and offer us any cakes. Perhaps he was making a special delivery of cakes for the Queen and did not have time to stop.

We waited and waited. We had a lookout and she could see right along the road towards the Lazy Corner, but even looking into the distance we could not see any vehicle coming.

Mary, from primary two, said she thought the Queen would go past in a gold carriage and that would have been fine, especially if it was pulled by white horses. But some of the older boys said the Queen only went in her horse-drawn carriage on special occasions. This was a special occasion for us and so I hoped she would appear in an open carriage.

Then a shout went up as a big black car was seen in the distance. The Queen! The Queen! It must be the Queen.

The big black car swept past us at one hundred miles per

hour, causing the flags and the little boys and girls holding on to them to ripple in its slipstream.

As we trudged back into school, I thought the Queen must have been late for her tea and sandwiches. I could understand that because if it had happened at my home, three small boys might well have eaten the sandwiches before she arrived.

Scrambling over History

I was looking at my comic, which was delivered every week in the same van as Dad's daily paper, when I read this story about how a big invading army attacked this castle. The people in the castle poured boiling oil down on the invaders as they tried to climb up the walls. There was also a drawing of a massive catapult which could hurl rocks at the walls of the castle and smash them. Another drawing showed a group of soldiers carrying their shields on their heads so that they looked like a big tortoise, but the real reason was not to imitate any animal but to stop them being hit by rocks and stones thrown down from the ramparts of the castle.

Now, we had a big castle not far from where we lived and it had big broken-down walls. I wondered if Ballinbreich Castle had been attacked by a big catapult and a huge army of people, some of whom were pretending to be a large tortoise.

Sadly, because this could have been really exciting, Dad said that our castle had not been built as a defence against marauding and aggressive armies or even pirates coming in from the mouth of the River Tay. I really still believed that our castle had been involved in a massive siege with boiling oil, catapults and cannonballs but Dad insisted that the Rothes family, who had built the castle with its wide red sandstone walls and massive baronial hall, really only wanted to impress the neighbours with their wealth.

He said the Barons of Rothes owned all the land around the castle and the farmers had to pay them rent. As a result of this money they were very rich. Mum said they were rich because one had married some rich heiress, but I don't know about things like that.

My brothers and I had never met anyone as important as a baron. For some reason there were no lords or barons or anything other than ordinary people at our little primary school. We did know that Dad had to pay rent to our new landlord and that he was an earl; the Earl of Zetland no less. But again we had never met him. He used to come around his properties once a year to check they were being well looked after and he was always accompanied by his estate factor. Mum and Dad had decided that it was too risky to let their often grubby and always inquisitive family into close proximity to the owner of the farm.

This was a pity because we had seen an earl in our comic books and he always wore purple robes lined with white fur. Sometimes earls carried big shiny swords. No one had ever worn white fur and ermine in our house, although we did have small wooden swords for fighting with. So, we small and seemingly un-presentable people were often sent away whenever there was 'a visit of the Laird.' One time we did see him as he came into the house and it was a surprise that he wore ordinary clothes with no ermine in sight.

Even if the earl was not as I had imagined and Dad had dismissed any idea of battles being fought at our castle, my brothers and I had to check it out just in case there were any old cannonballs or even empty vats that they had used for pouring boiling oil over people.

As we walked along the mile or so of the river's edge from our farm to where the castle stood, we discussed what it would be like to be a baron. I had been to a pantomime and I knew about Baron Hardup, but I noticed his castle was not made of big red sandstone walls. I wanted to say his pantomime castle walls flapped and shook a little when he shut his door but neither John nor Willie wanted to listen to me telling them that Baron Hardup had a pretty flimsy castle.

As we scrambled up the slope from the river towards the outside walls of the castle, we could not believe just how big it was. Compared to the farm workers' cottages, our farm house was big with two storeys, but this building was massive.

Hundreds of years had passed since the castle was lived in and undergrowth had grown up around the partially demolished sections of the walls with ivy and bramble bushes everywhere. We scrambled up some of the parts of the walls whose stones had been plundered by local farmers for building their new steadings.

Suddenly, as we pondered just how many rooms this castle would have, a great noise arose and the air around us grew dark. I cannot say I was always in favour of big brothers as they often made life difficult for me, but this was one occasion when I really was so happy that they were there. Our little expedition had disturbed the gathering of crows that lived in the trees around the ruins. The birds rose in one big black cloud and as they took wing, they gave out their loud, rough, cawing sound.

After they had gone, we slipped down off the walls and measured just how thick the builders had made them. Even when we extended our arms out to full stretch we could not touch both sides. The walls were so thick that Willie reckoned that even if the castle had come under fire from pirates and a cannonball had hit the walls, it would have pinged back and possibly killed some of the attackers.

I was none too keen to climb up the walls once more but the threat of being left behind was quite strong. So, shortly after my first fright with the crows, I scared myself again by climbing up and then looking down on the ground that seemed a long way below. It was far better to look up the river and see if there were any boats coming up to the local town. I suggested that if there had been such a vessel, we might have raised a pirate flag on the top of the ramparts of the old castle. This was dismissed, I think rather quickly, by both my brothers who no doubt realised that we did not have had such a flag or indeed the material to make one.

Then they told me that when the castle was lived in there was a secret tunnel between it and the local town. Sir William Wallace, one of Scotland's bravest men, had stayed in the castle before fighting a battle in the area and after the conflict, when he had had to escape, he used the secret tunnel. We started to look for it. I may say that John and Willie looked for the tunnel entrance with more enthusiasm than I did. I did not fancy going down into a dark tunnel and crawling on my hands and knees for two miles before emerging somewhere in Newburgh. I was also sure that if there was a tunnel, then I would meet rats and other creepy-crawly creatures that live in dark places and I had no wish to come face to face with them.

In fact, I was greatly relieved when both John and Willie decided they had had enough castle exploration for one day. We would come back another day, they promised, and I thought, they might, but I might be busy that day.

Worries about Harvest

LATE summer has always been a worry for me. Growing up on an arable farm, I could see the grain harvesting equipment being pulled out of the sheds and the men getting the binders ready for the coming harvest.

But I could also see the calendar on the wall in the kitchen and it was counting down the days to when I would have to go back to school. On the farm, the tractor drivers would go around pouring oil into the working parts of the harvesters and they would use grease guns in areas where I sometimes heard squeals of metal rubbing against metal. My brothers and I were warned not to go near the machinery because Mum did not like to wash trousers and shirts with oil or grease on them.

Dad would become increasingly agitated at harvest. Every day, it seemed, he would go round the fields checking to see if the wheat and barley crops were ready to cut. When we went with him, he would take a handful of the almost ripe heads and rub them in his hands so that the grains lay in his palm. He would then take one or two and bite them to see if they were hard and ripe. He told us it was no good if they were still soft and chewy. One day he gave a shout and a word I did not recognise as he bit the grain. Later he told Mum that he had broken a tooth and that the harvest would start that very day but he never told her the word he said when his tooth broke.

We followed the binders to the field because everyone on the farm was needed at harvest time, even small boys. I saw the easy job was sitting on the back of the binder pulling handles, but this job was left to the farm grieve and he sat there with the tractor and binder going round and round the field. He smoked his pipe as the machine spat out bunches of harvested grain. The hard work was done by the women who picked up these sheaves, one under each arm, and then put them together into little stacks of eight. After this had happened, the ground on which the crop had been grown was almost bare, apart, that is, from the roots and short stalks left below where the binder knives had cut. We played at pulling up this stubble and then making our own little stacks.

Or at least we did until a shout went up that there were rabbits coming out of the ever-reducing standing crop of grain. As the men cut round and round the field, the rabbits that had happily lived there eating my Dad's grain all season slowly retreated into a smaller and smaller area. Soon some came popping out and the men would stop what they were doing and chase them with sticks. The shepherd's dog also got in on the performance but he was a stupid dog and never caught one. Some men were better than others at this job as they seemed to know where the rabbits would run. Immediately the rabbits were killed, the men would slit open their tummies and take out all the long stringy puddings. After that they would tie two rabbits together by their back legs and hang them on the fence. Sometimes in fields that were close to woods where even more rabbits lived, there would be a whole row of dead rabbits by the time the field was finished. A man with a van would come at night and take them away, but most of the men took a pair of rabbits home for their supper.

Rabbit chasing was almost as thirsty work as harvesting and I noticed that everyone stopped when Mum arrived with a can that contained oatmeal and water. Sitting with our backs to one of the little stacks of sheaves which are called 'stooks', we watched the men and then the women drink this mixture. We knew if we waited we could get the dregs that contained all the soggy oatmeal. That was the best bit as far as I was concerned, but I was not going to let the men know that.

There was so much to do, harvest days passed like a flash and soon, with the setting sun beginning to hide behind the hills, we would all get on a trailer and go back to the farm.

I was always so tired that I do not think I ever heard the end of a bedtime story when the heat of harvest was on.

Snow, Deep Snow

THE first I knew about it was when I heard Dad down in the kitchen. It was cold and my brothers and I were still in bed. However, as I listened to the adult voices downstairs, I soon realised that Dad was not in the best of moods. In fact, he was complaining.

'The sheep will need extra feed,' he said, followed by, 'the hens' water troughs are all frozen up,' but the clincher for his little family listening to this was, 'we will need to get the snow plough out.'

'Snow! Snow!' I shouted and within seconds the three of us had our noses pressed to the window to see just how much snow had fallen. In reality it took a little while for us all breathing heavily on the glass panes to remove the lovely patterns of frost that always adorned the bedroom windows on cold mornings. Only after a bit of huffing, puffing and scraping at the frost-covered glass with our fingers could we look out of the windows and see the snow.

We could not see any red stone chips where the gravel lay

around the house, so we knew the snow was thick. Not as much, possibly, as the three feet deep that I suggested to my brothers, but enough to get out and personally check how far it would come up our wellies.

Normally we dawdled about before getting out of our warm pyjamas and into the cold clothes that lay at the end of the bed. On cold mornings such as this we would sometimes reach out and bring our day clothes into bed to warm them up before quickly jumping into them. I reckoned I could put my outside clothes on when I still lay in bed but that was not a very successful experiment as it was possible to end up with a corner of the sheet tucked into your trousers.

More often on cold mornings, we quickly scooped up our little bundle of clothes and rushed downstairs to the kitchen where the coal-fired cooker was always warm. Dad filled it with coal at night and then again in the morning before he went out to work. We could hang our about-to-be-worn clothes on the warm rail in front. Sometimes Mum had left what she called a clothes horse out, which was a very fancy name for a wooden frame on which she hung all our wet clothes. On the cold mornings we would open one of the oven doors and, with our bottoms getting a blast of hot air, we could ease ourselves out of our night attire. If secrets can be told, it was possible that if we were up early enough in the morning we could find Mum doing the same bottom-warming, clothes-changing trick.

But this snowy morning was different and our clothes were

thrown on with teeth clenched against their sudden but not lasting coldness.

Mum caught us before we escaped outside and ensured that we wore slightly more clothing than we had planned. It was obvious that she did not share our enthusiasm for this phenomenon of white frozen rain. But she did ask one of the farm workers if he could get our sledges down from the rafters of the tool shed where they had lain since the previous winter.

We had two sledges between us which should have prevented most fights, but unfortunately one sledge was much faster than the other. The speedy sledge was no more than a metal framework with a single plank of wood on top whereas the slower model had a complete wooden seated area and the sides down to the runners were also filled in with wood. Its big problem was that it always slewed to one side when we rattled down the slopes.

Where would we go? Well, the farm was built on a slope and the first runs were often just down the main farm close between the buildings. This was all right on a Saturday afternoon when there was little farm activity, but on working days it had a risk factor when there were tractors and implements being moved about the farm.

With a shortage of sledges, those who were waiting for a turn created a slippy path or slide. By packing the snow down and then propelling ourselves down the slope, we could slide quite a distance, that is, provided we did not lose our balance and crumple into the snow alongside. Some of us were better sliders than others and John showed that he could not only go down the slide standing upright with arms outstretched, but also by bending his knees and almost sitting down he could go down the slide as a 'wee man', or at least that is what he called it.

But Dad soon warned us that making the farm ground slippy was not a good idea, as older people not so hell-bent enthusiastic on slippy paths might come a cropper if they mistakenly put a foot on one of our slides.

The next move was up into the paddock above the road. This had an extra steepness to it and a reasonable turn of speed could soon be achieved. The only part that Mum did not like about this location was there was no slowing down area and the speeding sledges could easily ping right into the fence, which itself was better than going through it and then landing on the tarmac road. Willie proved this point by catching one of the fence wires with his nose on one occasion. He then left a trail of red blood-spattered snow as he staggered off for repairs. The trail he left was quite beautiful, but I do not think he thought so as he held on to his red nose.

That one accident apart, we soon became experts at either falling off just before hitting the fence or skewing the sledge around just before impact.

Other stunts soon followed. The fast sledge could hold all four of us and before Mum could do anything from her vantage point at the kitchen window her whole brood had launched itself down the slope towards the fence which was ever so slightly out of her vision.

By this time the other children on the farm had joined us and the loads on the sledges became heavier and I noticed that, when this happened, it also increased the speed of the downhill run.

The worst part was always pulling the sledge back up the hill. Once when Gina had a pony we thought we would enlist this one-horse power to help pull our sledge on the upward trip. This also meant, we thought, that we could jump aboard for the uphill ride. But the pony was not too keen on the idea and what with a bit of horsy reluctance and an impatience to maximise the time on the snow, the idea of using horse power was soon shelved.

Sometimes the older folk came along for the fun and we would watch as they found out the tricks we had invented all by ourselves without adults showing us what to do.

I wondered if perhaps they had also sledged and played in the snow when they were young.

Pocket Money Chickens

I do not think Mum ever did find out where her kitchen scales disappeared to every Saturday. Possibly she did, but she never revealed that she was in on our secret. Apart from anything else, the scales were always returned to her kitchen sideboard within an hour or two.

Not that it was a great secret. The fenced off part of the yard where my brothers, sister and I kept a batch of hens was quite open and the men on the farm could see what we were up to with our latest money-making ploy.

They witnessed the weekly weighing of our livestock enterprise. We knew that our fortunes depended on selling our poultry as fat as they could be for the Christmas market. In the impatient way that youngsters have, we wanted to know how much cash would be coming our way. So, we would weigh the chickens individually each week and record their weights, just to see how many ounces they had gained over the previous seven days.

It would have been easier if we could have just weighed all one hundred birds in one batch, but there was no machine around the farm that could deal with that number. The only way we could calculate how much we would make was if we added up the total weight and then multiplied it by the two shillings and sixpence per pound that we had received from the poultry monger the previous year.

To carry out the weighing, we had to have catchers and soon all of us, apart from my little sister Gina, were expert at clutching the legs of the hens and then carrying them upside down to the scales. Gina was the recorder and she had a little book to note down the individual weights. The hens soon became very well trained and they would lie on the scales as if this was part of their normal life.

I think it was Willie who suggested we should put rings on their legs according to the weights. He had seen hen rings hanging up unused in the farm tool shed. So, soon, all the big heavy birds had bright red rings on their legs. Those that were slightly lighter had yellow rings and another step down saw the birds wearing blue rings. If on the weekly weighing, a bird stepped up a weight band, then the rings were changed. I do not know if these leg decorations brought about a certain hierarchy in the hen coop but we had a great deal of fun carrying out the operation.

So far I have called our livestock 'hens', but that was not true. They were all cockerels. Initially we were allowed to keep the few male birds that the chicken sexer had missed when Dad bought day-old chickens.

Male birds are not welcomed in a commercial egg-laying business and so, each year, we would have a few cockerels. After Dad became convinced we could look after more than the dozen or so birds that came disguised as hens, he then bought us about a hundred cockerels every year and we looked after them from day-old chicks, right until they went into the crates en route to the poulterers.

They arrived on our farm in cute little cardboard boxes with about twenty-five little fluffy chirping birds per hay-lined box. Under supervision, we transferred them to a sawdust covered area that was kept warm by a paraffin heater. We fed them special chicken meal and were warned not to lift the lid of the heated area because they might become chilled and then die. Unfortunately one or two of the little fluffy animals always did die and part of our stock-keeping duties was to dispose of the carcasses in the nearby cattle court. We also had to check that there was no blood in their droppings as that meant they had a disease from which they could die.

Soon the chickens lost their fluffiness in their wing feathers, marking out their growth, and so just like human babies their diet changed. We would recycle household scraps and as the enterprise grew in size, we would boil large vats of potatoes for them. Funnily enough, they were like humans in that they often pecked the inside of the potato out leaving behind the shell-like skin.

As the weeks passed and Christmas approached, we began

to check the prices that would be paid, although it always seemed as if the price we received was less than we had worked out.

Perhaps, fattening cockerels was never going to make me a millionaire.

Dropping Stitches

MUM would always ask how we got on at school. Every night, as we sat around the kitchen table, she asked each of us – John, Willie, me and Gina – in turn what lessons we had been doing.

Mostly this was alright because, by the time it came to me, I had selected one or two subjects where my day's efforts had been reasonable. Thus, Mum never knew about my knitting experience.

It seemed as if the teacher wanted everyone, boys and girls alike, to know how to sew and knit. Previously, it had been good enough for us boys to be taught gardening, leaving the girls to the sewing and knitting. However, armed with several pairs of knitting pins and a similar number of balls of brightly coloured wool, Mrs Armstrong stated that everyone at school would learn how to knit. We would start by knitting a scarf, she said.

In order to help us, she soon cast on the first row and it looked very easy. Even the little phrase she kept repeating to herself, 'in, over, through and out' would not be difficult to learn, especially as I looked over at the girls in the class and their knitting pins were already clacking away at a good rate. But I did wonder why Anna kept her tongue sticking out when she was knitting. Maybe that helped people to knit, but I was not going to do the same.

Whether I had my tongue in or out, it soon became evident that I was not one of life's natural knitters. I would manage a few stitches and then sort of lose interest as there were other things going on in the classroom. I did ask Anna, who seemed to be well ahead of the rest of us, if she would mind doing a little bit of my knitting, but I don't think she had forgiven me for showing her what a Chinese burn was. It was not as if I had held her arm tightly when I twisted my hands quickly in opposite directions, but she still gave a squawk of pain.

By the time the teacher rang the bell for the end of school, I was no more than half way along the first row and even I have to admit that some of my stitches were rather saggy apart, that is, from the one or two that were missing altogether. Thankfully, I put my knitting in the box in the cupboard and hoped that the knitting experiment was over.

But no, the very next week, the teacher brought out the box and announced another period of knitting. I did receive a surprise because there was more knitting on my pins than I remembered and it was better than my ragged efforts. Any thought of a knitting fairy were dismissed when Mrs Armstrong came along and said she would be keeping an eye on me as my efforts the previous week had been very poor and she had had to sort them out. Incidentally, I thought, she always said she had to keep one eye on Ronnie, so now that she was keeping her other eye on me, this meant she did not have any eyes left for the rest of the school. But I decided this was possibly not the best time to ask her about the number of eyes she had.

There were to be twenty rows of plain knitting for one end of the scarf and after that she said we were to do a mixture of plain knitting and purl for the middle section, before finishing up with another twenty rows of plain knitting for the other end. I groaned. This was going to take years and years of my life and there were so many other things I really wanted to do. So week in week out, I sat and knitted a few stitches. Then the teacher would rip back my little achievements in order to pick up stitches and then she added another two or three rows.

Now, some scarves can be shorter than others. By the end of term and the end of the knitting experiment, Anna and some of the other girls were able to wear scarves that could go several times around their necks. My scarf with its bright red wool ensured the back of my neck was kept warm, but that was all.

Hunter-Gatherers

POSSIBLY the best time in the school year occurred when the teacher produced a large thermometer. This was not one of those little glass efforts that took your temperature when you put it under your tongue or in your armpit. (I did not believe Ronnie when he said the doctor sometimes put it up your bottom.) The school thermometer was a large paper one that hung on the wall behind the teacher's desk. On this, she would mark in red the pounds of rose hips that our little primary school collected. As the pounds of berries came in, the red ink rose.

As schoolchildren, we did not need a great deal of encouragement to use up our early autumn evenings or our weekends for picking hips. The reward was already there in the three pennies per pound that was paid for all the berries we had picked. We knew also that the school received an additional penny for every pound of berries that was collected and the money went into the school funds to help pay for the school Christmas party. We were also aware of our school's top reputation in rose hip collection. We collected more rose hips per pupil than any other in Fife, which was the whole world as far as we were concerned.

So as we walked the road to and from school we would look at the hedgerows and mark out the good bushes of hips, so that after we had thrown off our school clothes, we could return to start collecting the rosy red fruit. It was never a good idea to pick rose hips in your school jacket and trousers. The bushes were full of thorns that would quickly cause a tear, and a tear in our good clothes resulted in, at the very least, a scolding, as Mum was then required to get out her repairing needle and thread.

If the hip thorns were not bad enough on their own, the neighbouring hedge was also full of hawthorn and sometimes even very prickly blackthorn. We did not know then that the first livestock farmers to enclose their fields had no wire fences and instead they planted hedgerows of prickly bushes as these were ideal for keeping cattle and sheep in place.

So, now in our out-of-school hours and in our out-of-school clothes, we returned to the hip bushes. The older pickers and the more cunning ones had often borrowed their Dads' shepherd's crooks. Although my Dad was not a full-time shepherd, his walking stick with the special hooked handle could pull down the more difficult-to-reach branches which somehow always had more fruit on them. This 'pulling down' exercise brought its own troubles and there was often a tussle between the person bringing the berries closer to hand and the pickers. The holder of the stick soon realised he could not fill his basket with just one free hand and equally quickly he realised others were benefiting from his efforts. A formula had to be worked out to ensure a continuation of this co-operative picking system and, thereafter, we pickers agreed every third handful of berries had to be contributed to the 'puller down's' collecting basket.

We became experts in the varieties of hips. They might have been the same genetic family but they displayed widely differing characteristics. Some still had the husks attached but others had shed these. Some hips were large and round while others were oval. No matter, they all went into our baskets.

Soon all the roadside bushes were picked clean and we started to search further afield. Some ventured into Flisk Wood which lay just behind the school, but my brothers and I had, during the summer holidays, reconnoitred this particular area and could find no great number of bushes. A similar tale existed further along at Balhelvie Wood where there were some bushes but not enough to tempt my brothers, my sister and me.

Our favourite area was down at the riverside. Rose hip bushes seemed to like to grow beside the water. But, as we marched off on a weekend morning, we had to make sure that we did not just head straight to where we knew there were rich rose hip pickings to be had. Others might have seen us and thus deprived us of some of our earnings had they followed us. So a slightly circuitous route was taken before we ended up at the riverside. Soon my brothers and I were in an area where there were bushes with ripe berries all around. Willie reckoned this was a rose hip grove just as there were olive groves in the Bible. As he was bigger and as I did not know what an olive was, far less a grove, I took his word for it.

We had cheese and jammy pieces made up and bottles of water and lemonade so that we could work all day. As the oldest, John was generally left to decide when it was time to eat our food. He also warned us to hang our piece bags on fence posts and not leave them lying on the ground as mice would soon smell something nice and cheesy so they would try to burrow into the bags. He said he had seen the shepherd's dog pinch some of the men's pieces when they were working and that had caused a big row between the men and the shepherd.

We worked all day, although sometimes we played a little on the shore where there were always interesting things like dead seagulls and rubbish from ships being washed up. By the time we headed home, the various baskets and bags were teeming with ripe fruit. Even on days when the playing about had exceeded the time spent picking, it looked as if our baskets were spilling over with berries. Little did those who looked in amazement at our efforts know that the bottoms of the baskets were full of dry seaweed and there was only a little layer of rose hips covering the top.

On a Monday morning during rose hip picking season, there were not only the usual school bags to get ready, but we also had to take the red hips to be weighed. On those days, Mum or Dad would take us to school in the car, collecting others on the way, each with their closely guarded weekend's harvest. At school,

the teacher would bring out big brass scales and we would watch the weights being put on the other side to balance what we had collected. Once weighed, the berries went into small jute sacks, each holding twenty-eight pounds. A stack of these was then left in the school porch ready for collection by a small lorry.

It was the end of the season before we were paid for our picking efforts and often Dad insisted that we transfer the money straight into National Savings Certificates which cost £1 each. So, apart from the loose change, our picking efforts brought no immediate wealth.

Mind you, I did not even know why we were picking these red berries. Right from my earliest memories, I had seen bottles of rose hip syrup in Mum's medicine cabinet. When any of the family was poorly, this would be the bottle that was pulled out and a spoonful of the sickly, sweet fluid administered to whoever was ailing.

I read the instructions on the side of the bottle and found out that the contents were bursting full of Vitamin C. Apart from keeping sailors travelling to faraway lands free from scurvy, I did not know what Vitamin C did for anyone. I knew that I had often been called scruffy, but I did not think that this was the same disease as scurvy.

I remained blissfully ignorant until I came to the bit on the label that said rose hip syrup was good for expectant mothers. I did not know what 'expectant' meant and wondered if this applied to Mum as I had seen her take some spoonfuls. As someone who was always encouraged to ask questions when-ever I did not know something, I queried whether Mum was an expectant mother. I remember this innocent question getting hoots of derision from my older brothers who seemed to know something I did not. Mum smiled and said nothing and I do not recall getting an answer to my query.

But I do know that I never did get any more brothers or sisters, despite Mum taking a spoonful of rose hip syrup every now and then.

The Daily Trek

WHEN you have short legs, and my legs were quite short when I started primary school, walking one mile is quite a distance. It is an even bigger journey if there are distractions and diversions along the route. For the little gang of pupils who walked from my Dad's farm to the school, there were always lots of things that prevented us getting to school as quickly as our parents planned.

So in the morning the school teacher would be out ringing her bell even before we went around the Lazy Corner which was still some distance from the school. Having been called lazy both by my Mum and by the teacher, I wondered why this part of the road was also called lazy. It had no homework to do. It had no work to do. It was just there doing nothing. So why, I wondered, did it have such a name? Dad knew and told me that in the olden days when horses went along that way, they would prefer to walk a slightly longer way, sticking to the contours of the ground, rather than dipping down into the small valley and then having to climb back up again.

Sometimes at the other end of the day, Mum would be looking out for us but the homeward journey was nearly always quicker. My older brother, Willie, said this was because it was downhill but I thought it had more to do with tea being ready and games waiting to be played.

The length of the journey also depended on the season. In winter, unless there was snow which would definitely cause a snowball fight diversion, the trip was generally as fast as our legs could carry us. Apart from possibly seeing the men out ploughing the fields or spreading dung, there was little reason to stop and look.

However, in spring and summer we often dawdled along the same route. There were so many distractions. Spring time was seeding time and everyone in the country seemed to be happier. The men would be working with cultivators and seeders. Later in the season, when the crops started growing, they would be singling sugar beet so that each root grew to its maximum size. Another job they did was picking stones off the land so that when harvest came, the machines would not break down by hitting a big one. When the men saw us, they would shout, telling us we would be late for school but I do not think our little gang that walked from my Dad's farm ever upped our tempo as a result of these encouraging words.

If it was wet or if there was a special reason to complete the trip in fast time, we would walk the distance between one telephone pole and the next and then run between the next poles, alternating throughout the one-mile trip or at least until such time as the girls or the smaller kids dropped off the back and started squawking about being left behind. Our mums and dads had warned us to keep together, otherwise there would be ructions when we arrived at our destination.

Sometimes I just walked behind the rest and looked up at the sky and wondered about the clouds. On sunny days they went away as high as I could see and lay there in big white crinkled sheets. On dull days, they turned grey and fluffy and they came down towards where we were walking. Some days they came right down and we could not see the school or even the next telephone pole. I wondered what it would be like to be above the clouds and decided I would be a pilot when I grew up so that I could find out.

On very wet days we were excused the walk so we waited until the postman came in his little red van. Then we would bundle ourselves into the back part of the van before swinging the big metal lever that held the door shut. We saw the piles of letters he had to deliver and we waited as he stopped at various houses on the road before he dropped his passengers right at the school door. On those wet days, Mrs Armstrong allowed us to go into the classroom even if it was still playtime. She said she did not want a school full of damp, smelly children. I could understand why she said damp but never worked out why she thought we were smelly.

Another reason for not walking too fast towards school was that there were nests in the hedgerows that ran alongside the road. In winter, with the leaves off and the branches bare, we could see where the old nests had been. But the clever part came in the spring when we would watch where the mother blackbird, thrush, yellowhammer or bullfinch swooped around protectively as we neared her nest. We soon found out that if you stood quite still and did not make a noise, the mother bird would lead you there. Then we would hold back the branches of the hedge and look in to see how many eggs she had laid. We never took any eggs because we knew that as the days went past we would be able to see the young birds as they emerged from the shells. Sometimes, though, we saw dead little birds lying on the roadway after falling out of their nests. There they were, all skinny and bare. Or they were until the crows swooped down out of the sky and picked the little bodies up and ate them.

I know that on the farm my Dad had a big wire cage in which he caught any crows that came to eat eggs that the farm hens laid. I hoped the cage would catch the crows that ate the little blackbird chicks.

One day, as we walked to school, we saw a mother weasel lead her pencil-thin brood across the road in front of us, but we did not even try to have a closer look at them. We had all heard the squeals of pain that came from a rabbit which had been caught by a weasel. My brothers and I had also seen the damage they could cause to the inhabitants of a hen house. After picking up dozens of dead hens after a weasel attack Dad called these little animals 'blood-thirsty killers.'

But it was autumn time that we liked best. There were berries in the hedgerows and these were there to be collected or, in the case of brambles, tasted. We knew where the juicy berries were and even if it meant a slight detour into the fields on the other sides of the hedges that was permissible.

I do not think the teacher ever found out that we had been picking brambles but Mum did ask why we had wide red bramble juice streaks all around our mouths. Some days when we tired of eating berries, we would jump over the fence and pull a turnip from the field. Then we would hold the turnip over our heads before smashing it down on the road and picking up some of the little pieces of fresh root which were very good to eat.

Depending on the time of year, we would often stop to talk to Willie, who worked as a roadman. In the summer he would cut the grass on the verges, leaving it in lines along the bankings. He used a big scythe. Rather than take this home every night on his bicycle, he would hide it in the hedge or behind a tree. We knew this but we had been warned never to touch the scythe as it could easily cut off our arms or legs, it was so sharp.

In the winter, he would trim back the hedges and he had a special long-handled knife that he used for this job. When he was finished the hedges were very neat and tidy.

Willie was always happy when we talked to him and I wondered about becoming a roadman when I left school. It was either that or being a pilot.

Pay Day

IT was a chilly October morning and it was still half dark outside. Inside the house there was turmoil; the sort of turmoil that is created when there are four children getting ready to go out for a day picking potatoes.

One brother accused another of pinching his gloves, a much needed accessory for anyone hand-picking potatoes. Then Mum accused me of wearing a pair of trousers that were still good enough for school use. Gina was looking for a scarf that had last been used some six months earlier in the cold March winds.

Mum was busy making the all-important food parcels or 'pieces'. We had been warned there would be no running back to the house for breakfast or even for lunch. Breakfast was being made with slices of white bread and lovely rosy red raspberry jam. Lunch looked to be shavings of hard Cheddar cheese, which was the only cheese that ever existed, and again this was clamped between two pieces of white bread. There was another slight squabble as it seemed to me that I was getting all the ends of the loaves and as everyone knows, these ends or heels, were often far more difficult to bite through. Throughout all this hurry and scurry, Dad kept popping his head around the door wondering if we were ready.

Eventually, swaddled in layers of clothing, we joined the rest of the local picking gang who were going out to the field on the back of a trailer. Happily, we bounced along the track to the field. We could see the farm lorry with its high sides on. These sides were normally used only when transporting cattle and sheep to market, but today the lorry was unloading a crowd of people. We had seen the farm grieve get the lorry ready the previous day. He had lowered the high or float sides, as they were called, on to the flat platform and then he had laid out a row of straw bales down either side. Thus it was ready to go into Newburgh, the local town, to collect a potato-picking squad.

The rows of potatoes looked long and we could see the farm grieve, having delivered his squad, now go to the edge of the field where he broke off a few branches of an ash tree. Then, with a big armful of these branches under his arm, he started walking up the rows, placing one of these markers every few yards. These denoted our starting and finishing points for picking. My two older brothers had decided they could pick a whole bit, or length, between them. My little sister and I were told before we left the house, to ask for only a half-bit between us.

Before the digger came around spinning the potatoes out of the drill, this length seemed very small. But after the tractor had passed, we realised there were a lot of potatoes to gather up into the cane baskets. We picked all the potatoes in our section and were quite happy until we saw the digger coming around again for a repeat performance. So we bent our backs and filled our baskets the second time. Now the tractor driver seemed to be going faster and faster. Further up the field, the boys from the local town were shouting rude things at him but he smiled and paid no attention. He possibly even went faster than ever.

Meanwhile, the grieve kept moving the sticks across the field and, as the field was not square, the bits were getting bigger, or at least I was sure the little bit my sister and I shared was now much larger. Some of the layers of clothing were cast off as we were no longer cold. Earlier, some boys had gathered together withered potato tops and had used them to make a fire, but this fire was mainly to bake potatoes for their breakfast.

Not content with making the bits bigger, the grieve patrolled the field going up and down expertly kicking over any divot where he thought an unpicked potato may have been hidden. I thought of the story my Dad told of his father kicking over the divots looking for potatoes and finding instead a rat which then proceeded to crawl up his trouser leg. Rather cautiously, I checked to see there were no potatoes left under the divots in the area Gina and I were responsible for. By this time she had started complaining about being tired and she wanted to start eating her piece but Mrs Nicol, the grieve's wife, who was on the next bit, would not allow such an indulgence.

When the break eventually came we sat on the upturned baskets and ate as if we had not eaten for a whole week. We looked at the remainder of our little pack of food and wondered if we could not just eat it all, but John said no. We tried not to think about the two and more hours that existed before we could next have a rest at lunchtime.

Shortly afterwards, there was an argument with our brothers on the next bit. We thought they were cheating by not starting to pick right across from the marking stick. We scuffed the drills to make our point and then they scuffed the drills in their favour; it did no good other than to pass the time.

As our backs started to ache we tried other picking methods; instead of the stooped approach with the basket between our legs, we crawled along on our knees – but the only thing that this proved was that it was slower than the original way.

We watched in amazement the older boys from Newburgh picking their bit quickly and then running behind the trailer into which the baskets were emptied; they would hitch a ride up the field on this, chatting to their friends on the way.

Lunchtime came and with it an urn of hot tea which had been made in the farmhouse. Everyone filled their flasks and, sitting down on upturned baskets, took their break.

As the food supply in our school bags dwindled away, the only thought that kept us going was the cash we would get at the end of the day. We started to count how many more times the digger would come around. We cheered when it hit a rock and the driver had to get down off the tractor to see to the stone stuck in the digger. He had a big hammer in his hand and he walloped away at the rock until it broke into small pieces. Having freed the machine, he started up again with what I thought was determination to catch up the lost time.

We wondered about sitting in the drills in front of the tractor in order to stop it but decided against this because the driver's eyesight was not as good as it might have been and even if he had seen us, he might not have been able to stop as quickly as might have been necessary.

Somehow we got through the day. Further up the field there were noticeably fewer high jinks in the afternoon. There was less running about the field chasing the girls with mice that had been tumbled unceremoniously out of their little nests by the digger. There was also less throwing half-cooked potatoes at each other.

We saw Dad arrive in the Land Rover and that meant only one thing: it was time to receive our pay. He started at the top end of the field and marched down handing each picker a small brown pay envelope which was rapidly opened and checked. Down the field he came and soon there was only his own family waiting for a reward for their labours.

'I will see you lot later,' he said and that was that. There was disappointment that we were not treated the same as the rest of the squad, but our now extremely grubby faces hid that emotion.

After the last row had been dug, we dragged our weary bodies onto a trailer full of potatoes heading back to the farm steading where they would be stored. I was sad that I did not get a pay packet but I had heard Dad tell Mum that the price of potatoes was not good that year. So I just sat and thought sad thoughts.

Later, as we sat quietly around the tea table telling Mum stories of the day, Dad disappeared. On his return he handed each of us a pay packet with our name on it. It is no longer a secret, so I can tell you that each packet contained slightly more than we had actually earned.

Lessons at School

'NOW, if we take away another three, how many are left?' the teacher asked. I was reasonably good at arithmetic and the answer was easy. There had been eight used shotgun cartridges on my school desk and with two lots of three having been taken away, there were only two still standing on it. When Mrs Armstrong turned her back to attend to another pupil in her one-teacher school, I picked one of the empty shotgun cases up to see if it still smelled of cordite.

As someone brought up in the country, I knew this smell that came just after the shotgun had gone off. When Dad went out to shoot rabbits that had broken through the wire netting fence and were now eating his young crop of barley, I would go with him and pick up the spent cartridges and they all smelled of cordite. Later in winter, my brothers and I would sometimes come across a hide made out of branches of broom. Local shooters would use this hide on frosty days in winter when the geese came winging in from across the sky to feed on Dad's wheat crop.

There were always lots of empty cartridge cases lying around these hides and we used to pick them up. Cartridges were not just good for counting, as Mrs Armstrong found them, but we also used them as fences for our own toy farm.

There were other secrets in the teacher's cupboard at our school. There was a big pile of Plasticine that, early in the school year, had been in bright-coloured strips of yellow, blue and red, but now after a number of grubby hands had played with it and mixed it all together, was just a grey squidgy mass.

There was a box of old chestnuts which, again, the school used for counting. The boys at school could never understand where our teacher had collected these chestnuts from as there were no chestnut trees in our parish. In the autumn, my brothers and I hoped Mum, Dad or Aunt Jeanna would take us by car over to the village of Luthrie where there were several big trees that always had lots of chestnuts. Well, not always, because the local Luthrie boys also knew where the chestnut trees were and we could see where they had thrown sticks at the lower branches to get the big nuts.

My older brother John was the expert at making a hole in the chestnut with a hammer and nail so that I could thread through a piece of string from Mum's bag where all the little bits of string salvaged off parcels were kept. Then we fought conker contests, holding a conker on the end of a string while your opponent tried to smash it. It was then your turn to try and smash his puny little conker and this went on until one of the conkers was broken into little bits. I was never very successful, although I did once have a ten-ser. Not many people I spoke to knew that this meant it was a chestnut that had smashed ten others.

We only played conker fights for a short period every year. Most of the time we played football on our own steep little school playground with its worn-out tarmacadam surface. Football has many rules but the first and most important one for me and the rest of Flisk school was 'Do not fall'. We all knew that falling was painful. It left bloody knees full of little pieces of grit. In a few days, the bloody bits turned into black scabs which Mum said I was not to pick even if they were very, very itchy.

Being in the playground was much better than doing classes, except when the gym teacher came to visit our school. She wore a short black skirt and neither I nor any other of my pals had ever seen so much bare leg, or at least as much bare leg that did not have scabs on them. So I do not know where the gym teacher played football.

We also had an art teacher who came around in a big old car and he taught us how to draw and paint which was good fun as it was much easier than trying to learn spelling, geography or history. He asked us if we knew about perspective and of course none of us did, but he painted a big man in the front of his picture and a small man at the back and said that was perspective. I was going to ask if the front man was just big and the other man was just small. But Mrs Armstrong was already looking cross as she sat at her desk watching her class so I decided I would wait until another time to ask about big and little people and their perspective on things.

If there is a list of things I do not understand about school, then singing would be almost at the top. Singing itself was not bad because I soon found out you did not have to make a noise, it was much easier just to pretend to make a noise. Most of the time I could just move my lips without singing, but Mrs Armstrong would sometimes walk in front of me and listen to see if there was any noise coming from my direction. Apart from that, the strange part about our singing lessons was that the whole school would be made to sit around a wireless in the school and listen to this special singing programme. Then we would have to sing to the wireless and the man on the wireless said our singing was very good. When I tried talking to the wireless in our kitchen, Mum made a funny face and laughed when I told her the man on the wireless could hear me.

Sometimes I think schools are not the best places to learn about important things such as talking to wirelesses.

Reporting Back

FOR most of the time, the last week of school before summer holidays was good fun. There was more time for playing and Mrs Armstrong seemed quite relaxed about small people talking in her school.

I started to think of all the things that I could do in the weeks ahead, and school lessons were definitely not on that list.

However, as is often the case, there was a little black cloud looming over my horizon. Well, it was not black. Report cards, or progress cards as they were optimistically called, came in a little beige coloured book. Without saying a word, Mrs Armstrong went down the rows of desks handing them out. Like all the rest of the pupils in her little school, I knew that in between the covers of the little book was her verdict on our individual performances over the past term. I knew that getting an 'A' against a subject was good and that an 'E' was not good. Not that I ever had any 'A's, but some of my friends used to get them and they seemed to be delighted by this single letter of the alphabet.

The real problem was the space at the bottom where a parent

or guardian had to sign it as proof that the report card had been taken home.

I used to leave it on my desk unopened for as long as possible, hoping that it would be better than I feared. Gently I opened it to read the verdict. It said quite simply 'A slight improvement.'

That was, I thought, a pretty good comment. After checking with my classmates, I worked out that I was fourth in my class. So, as I walked and ran home that night, I was really quite happy.

'A slight improvement' I thought, and if I held it correctly when showing it to Mum and Dad, my finger could cover up the 'slight' leaving them to read 'improvement.' It was positive and I would tell them I was fourth in my class.

It was my older brother, Willie, who cast the first shadow over my optimism. 'You were not fourth. You were second last.' Arithmetically, he was, I suppose, correct, as there were only five in my class, but with three swotty girls, I was the first boy, having gained more marks than Ronnie.

Then my other brother, John, decided to look more closely at my report. He read out, 'A poor report' which was how teacher had described my first-term efforts. Then, picking up a theme, he read out, 'A disappointing report' as the verdict on my second term. 'So it is just not as bad as the other two', was his cruel jibe. By this time we were nearly home and there was no escape, short of just dying, and I did not fancy that with seven weeks of holiday on the horizon.

Without commenting on it, I just left the report card where Mum would find it. Miraculously, not a word was said and when I picked it up next morning, it was signed ready to be returned to school.

Perhaps Mum knew how difficult it was being at school.

Sports Day

I do not know why the teacher picked David and me for the important job of carrying the bucket of water along to where the school was going to hold its Sports Day.

We had been playing, or as Mrs Armstrong called it 'messing about', when she asked us to go down to where the school meals were served. There we would get a large galvanised pail which we had to fill with water and then take along to the sports field. Mrs Armstrong may have called it a sports field but it was not really, because Mr Noble still had his cows in it.

David and I were good friends, but the teacher must have known that sharing the carrying of a pail of water puts a strain on any relationship. Only a few steps into the journey, David accused me of holding my side of the pail too high so that water slopped down his leg. Just to prove how this was done, he lifted his side of the pail and water did indeed run down my legs and onto my socks which were new on that very day.

We put the pail down to discuss the matter and decided that we had filled it far too full in the first place, so we tipped a lot of it out. It was now much lighter and we could, if we were careful, actually run with the pail between us. But this soon stopped because the water was again escaping. Only this time, both of us were getting wet.

Although we had been allowed out ahead of the rest of the school, they were now catching up with us. We stood at the side of the road and watched them go past but we both reckoned it was too dangerous to try and flick them with water from the bucket, because Mrs Armstrong was marching along behind the little crocodile of children.

After looking at how little water was now left in the pail, she placed David and me just in front of her for the rest of the forced march.

As soon as we entered the field, Mr Noble's cows came around. Cows are always curious, I knew from going out with my Dad on the farm. With their big, sad eyes and their soft, wet noses, whenever you went into a field they would always nudge up as if they were looking for food. This was alright for the rest of the school, but they seemed to think that we had brought them something special in the bucket, so David and I had to do a great deal of shooing and shouting at them to keep them at bay. I think the teacher kept close behind us because she had not been brought up on a farm and was not sure of what cows were like.

By this time the school cleaner arrived and she was carrying old sacks, skipping ropes and some of the spoons from the school kitchen. So we had races. Some of them were just straightforward races. I did not win because the girls were always given a start. We had sack races and we could all smell they had been used for potatoes. The next event was difficult. The teacher called it a three-legged race. I thought it would have been good if you could have chosen your other leg and a half for this race but the teacher was in charge and she tethered me to Mary who was really quite slow when it came to running. So that was another race I did not win.

We had, in fact, been so busy running that we had quite forgotten about the pail of water. We were all asked to sit down in a circle around the bucket and then, from deep inside the big bag that she always carried, the teacher produced a packet of Creamola Foam. Occasionally, I could persuade Mum to buy us a packet and my brothers, sister and I were allowed a glass of this fizzy sugary drink. But a whole packet of the lemon flavour, which was my favourite, went into the pail. We all sat around and took turns dipping a cup into the foaming brew.

Then, to make it even better, the school cleaner produced a basket full of sandwiches. Some of these had cheese in them, but most were full of scrunchy lettuce. We sat there eating them as the cows circled around wondering why we were eating and they were not.

The empty bucket was much easier to carry back to the school and, as David and I took a side each, I wondered why we did not have Sports Day every day.

A Healthy Diet

EATING is quite funny. Not that it makes you laugh. It is just that some things can make you hungry and others do not. I could be sitting at a lunch which Mum had made and looking at the potted head or the corned beef and thinking I was not very hungry. Yet, a few minutes afterwards I would be eating bits of raw turnips. After picking away at my plate, Dad would suddenly announce, 'Come on, I need a helper to feed the sheep.' Now that may have sounded like he needed a volunteer, but what that meant was 'You are coming with me to help chop up the turnips for the sheep.'

So with wellies, old coats and a woolly balaclava helmet, I would soon be struggling to keep up with Dad as he splashed across the muddy, wintry field where the sheep were being fattened for the market. As I hurried along behind, he explained that the sheep would eat more turnips if they were all sliced up and that is what we were going to do. There was a heap of turnips and just beside it was an old machine that cut them up. Taking the machine covers off, he picked up a handle and was soon turning it around to get the mechanism cranked into life.

My part, and a critical one at that, was to hold this lever up until the precise moment when Dad grunted 'let it go.' To be honest, I let it go too late the first time and then the next time I was too early which Dad, who was now breathing heavily with the exertion of turning the handle, did not seem to appreciate. At that point I might well have been made redundant if he had had a third hand. But he didn't and on the third attempt I dropped the lever at the precise moment and the turnip cutter engine spluttered into life.

My job was to throw the turnips into the big cutting drum and he would carry the end product to the sheep who, by now, were all gathered around. In fact, they were not just gathered around waiting. Some were pushing others out of the way and I was glad to be on the side of the wire netting away from them, as even Dad was pushed by some of the bigger, bolder ones. Keeping the machine full of turnips was warm work and soon old coats and hats were being taken off. But the bit I was going to tell you about was when Dad was away with a basket of cut turnips, I sneaked around and chose one of the less muddy slices for myself. It was ever so slightly earthy but I did wipe it on my trousers before taking a bite of it.

I do not know why Mum never gave us raw turnip for lunch because it tasted really good.

The Toy Shed

I cannot really remember, but I think it all started during one of those times when Mum decided that the house needed a big clean. She called it a spring clean, which was different from all the tidying that went on every year just after Christmas.

It was the spring cleaning that seemed to involve a lot of hard work, with sheets and blankets being stripped off beds and big washings going out on the clothes lines. It was not just in the bedroom that there was turmoil as every room in the house seemed to have to be dusted and polished from top to bottom. I do know it was not a good time to be a small boy as you could easily get roped in to help fold sheets, carry heaps of washing upstairs and downstairs, as well as a lots of little jobs for which there was no pay.

Worse than that there was no peace. No sooner had I got my toys scattered over the kitchen floor or on the stairs than Mum would scoop them to one side, saying that I was always under her feet. On more than one occasion, she destroyed a whole farmyard and she also reduced a house I was building to the rubble of a few blocks of wood.

That was possibly why, soon after, I saw the local joiner out in the garden building a little wooden shed. Within days it was completed and no sooner had that happened than my brothers, sister and I found all our toys moved out to this new extension of our house.

I grumbled a bit because the hut was always cold, but Dad put in a paraffin heater and that made it better. We then found that we each had a drawer where we could keep our own toys. This was good as we did not want Gina's dolls mixing with our farm livestock or our cowboy clothes. But it was also bad as I reckon I lost some of my toys that found themselves in my brothers' belongings. It was worth a fight, but they pointed out after I had been beaten that they had just allowed me to play with their toys.

So, on any wet day when we could not get out to the farm, we ended up in the new wooden hut and Mum was left in her now much tidier house. We still played some games in the house as there was a bench on which we sat at mealtimes which, when one end was lifted onto the sideboard, made an excellent chute. Sometimes, however, it left a splinter of wood in a small person's rear end. There were always the banisters which we would slide down hoping that, if we fell, it would be onto the stair side as plunging the other side down into the hallway involved a certain amount of sudden stopping and pain.

There was also a certain amount of traffic between the house and the hut. Important toys such as boxes that once held oranges or dates were needed to make farm buildings. Mum's string bag was also borrowed on several occasions, as fences had to be made to keep our little tin animals from wandering out of fields.

What we did not have was a machinery repair centre. It was great to get the latest Dinky tractor with its body painted blue, red or grey, depending on its type and it looked good with its black tyres. Well, it looked good until Gina found out that she could remove the tyres and then stick them in her mouth and either chew them to bits or just eat them. I knew without even asking the men on the farm that tractors without tyres are pretty useless things.

So, unfortunately, parts of my farm yard looked a little like a scrap yard for old vehicles.

Pets

HE was 'flat as a pancake' said Bob, one of Dad's tractor men. I knew what he meant, but I did not want to think about it, as Bob was describing how my pet cat, Tam, was last seen lying spread-eagled across the road, no longer thinking of chasing mice or little birds.

I had been told that cats have nine lives, but Tam had just used up his whole quota in one go as he had been hit by a car travelling past the farm. I thought sad thoughts. There would be no more picking up my big tom cat and listening to his happy purring as I held my ear to his rib cage. It sounded just like one of Dad's tractors when it was being driven along the road. There would be no more tying a big knot at the end of a piece of string and wiggling it along the floor to get Tam to pounce on it in a cat-like manner. In short, there would be no more Tam.

The tractor man buried him in the dung midden in the farm stackyard, but I did not go to the funeral. Nobody went other than the tractor man. It might seem a funny place to bury a cat, but often if the ground was frosty, as it was when my cat was killed, it was easier to dig up some of the soft warm dung than it was to dig a hole in the frozen ground.

Dad never said, but I do not think he was too sad about there being no big tom cat around the house. One day as he was eating his porridge, Tam had jumped onto Dad's back and this caused quite a disruption for a while as Dad chased the cat around the kitchen and then out of the door.

For the next few weeks, there were no cats allowed in the house. However, I knew that cats were quite sly, sneaky animals and soon they would sidle in when Dad was not around. Before long they were curled up in front of the cooker as if nothing had happened.

But that was long before Tam was 'pancaked' and now there was no more Tam. There was never another Tam. His sister, Rainbow, did produce litters of new kittens and one of those, Ginger, was my favourite for a while, but Ginger was more my sister Gina's cat.

My friend, David, never did have a cat. His family had a big dog. It was not a shaggy sheepdog, it was big and brown and it sprawled lazily in front of the fire. I do not know if I can tell you this, but when it lay there, it made smells. It did it quite quietly, not like some of the boys at school who could make noisy smells. We thought this was funny but David's Mum and Dad never laughed, although sometimes his Dad pulled the news-paper right up in front of his face, so we could not tell.

We did have a dog called Ben on the farm. He was supposed

to be a sheepdog but I do not think he ever worked out how to shepherd sheep. The shepherd would shout 'way by, Ben', meaning he was to go out and circle the sheep, but Ben never did go 'way by.' After some shouting, Ben would decide that it would be easier if he just went back to his kennel and that is what he did. At this point the shepherd would look around and see if anyone else would volunteer to go 'way by' and his eye alighted on my brothers and me who were watching.

Being sheepdog substitutes is not too bad and it makes you really fit. Some days when we were moving the sheep along the road, we would be used as 'gate fillers' which is what we called running ahead and then standing in each open gateway to prevent the sheep taking the wrong road. If you let any sheep past you when you were on guard duty, you got a row. Not too bad a row, but still a row. Once the flock was past, you had to then run through the fields to get in front for the next gateway.

That is why Dad's farm never had a sheepdog, or a proper one anyway.

The Great Expedition

TO this day, I cannot recall just how the seed was sown. Was it Mother, tired of her three sons romping through her house some three weeks into the summer holidays, or was it one of my older brothers, wanting to spread his wings by travelling beyond the immediate horizons of the farm?

I do know that I was not the prime mover of the idea that would see my two brothers and I cycle along to my Granny's house in Wormit, some ten miles closer to the Tay estuary.

A few months earlier, I had woken on my eleventh birthday to find that a Raleigh bicycle had come gleaming into my life. The bike was sturdy. Its main frame was black, as all bicycles seemed to be in those 1950s days and the chrome handlebars shone brightly. To begin with, the seat was as low as it could go so that my feet could touch the ground. As the years passed and my legs grew longer, the saddle would be gradually raised. It was wonderful, although I was sad that my new bike did not have a three-speed gear change like my friend David's. I did mention this failing to Dad, but he assured me that I had many more than just three speeds in my legs. He said I could cycle very slowly if I wanted to or if I was hurrying then I could pedal very fast and I could go at any speed in between if I liked. There was therefore no need for an expensive gear change on my bike. That issue having been sorted out, my thoughts transferred to the big journey itself.

There was, if I recall, some disagreement over who should carry the picnic that we planned to have en route. As the smallest person on the expedition, I had a slight fear that the rations might not be divided equally. However, John was entrusted to carry the haversack and also to see that the food was shared out between the team.

We did not leave until after lunch and the plan was to complete the journey in time for tea at Granny's house. Dad would come along with little sister Gina to collect the bikes and bring us boys home in the evening.

The road running through the middle of the farm is fairly flat so, full of enthusiasm and equally full stomachs, we raced along the initial part of the journey. Traffic was not heavy. We almost knew when vehicles would come along. The travelling vans worked to a timetable and we knew we might meet the bakery van. The post van had been, as had the milkman, and the butcher's van would not come until the next day. A public bus service only operated on one weekday, Tuesday, which was market day in Cupar, but it did also run on both Saturday and Sunday. The vehicles we had to watch out for were the travelling salesmen, who came around the farms selling fertiliser and seeds and buying grain and potatoes, but they never travelled fast along the country roads. These men always seemed to have heads like revolving lighthouses, taking in all the details of the crops so that when they spoke to the farmers they could do so with a degree of knowledge.

Like many other major expeditions, our trip soon hit problems. For some reason I cannot explain, older brother John decided to head us up Fliskmillan brae instead of taking the more direct route to Wormit. This steep road is a challenge and we were not long in getting out of the saddles and off the bikes, pushing and puffing. I was soon at the back of the trio and my bike had moved quickly from being sturdy to just plain heavy. Halfway up, we stopped to look back. We admired the holes in the hedge at the foot of the steep hill where various vehicles had failed to control their speed and thus ended up in the field below. We had heard the story of the minister's wife. She had not only overshot the junction into the field, but after plunging through the hedge, had then somersaulted her car twice before it had landed back on its wheels. To the amazement of the locals, she had then driven out with, as one observer noted, 'her hat still firmly in place.'

In similar fashion to almost every hill in life, Fliskmillan has a number of false summits. Several times we promised ourselves we would take another fifty steps and then it would all be level. Several times we were disappointed to see yet another rise to be conquered.

After what seemed a very long time, we crested the final brow and, mounting our sturdy steeds, we were soon moving fast towards a destination planned by John, but not revealed to the rest of the small expeditionary force.

Brunton lies in a hollow. It is a small hamlet where, uniquely, the householders all owned a small section of land. But it was not this feature that was in John's mind. It had a shop. Now, we were not used to shops. There was not a shop in the parish of Flisk where we lived. Messages came by van or from shopping trips to Newburgh some four miles away. But Brunton had a small shop. Some might have thought that the range of goods was extremely limited, but there was a tray of assorted sweets as well as a wooden crate with lemonade bottles. No doubt there were other things for sale in the shop, but the eyes of small boys do not get far beyond these goodies.

I was looking for one of those bags of potato crisps where the salt came in a little blue wrapping, but I do not think these had reached Brunton. So, weary from our efforts, we sat down on the bank of the burn that runs through the village and drank the lemonade. Safe from Mother's disapproving eyes, we drank straight from the bottle, or at least we did so after John, using his superior strength, flipped over the wire-bound stopper.

Suitably refreshed, we headed off. The difficult part was behind us as the road had no more than a series of gentle undulations, which provided little in the way of a challenge for us experienced bikers.

We scooted through the village of Gauldry. There was a minority cry for another stop, as this village also had a shop. However, my brothers decided to press on and, not wanting to be left behind, I stuck gamely to the task.

Wormit, our destination, came into view and with the finish in sight my older siblings raised the tempo, leaving me gasping along in the rear.

Thankfully, though I am not sure that is the right word, they stopped to allow me to catch up. Well, I was wrong, they did not; they stopped because they wanted to take a short cut. Our Aunt Jeanna, who could be counted on to lead us astray whenever we met, had once taken us on this track which included a tunnel that went under the main Dundee to Kirkcaldy railway line. Even on bright days there was a darkness about this part of the short cut. To give it a further edge in our minds, Aunt Jeanna said it was called the 'Rats' Tunnel'. Youthful imagination caught fire and soon we saw lots and lots of scurrying animals in the semi-darkness, or at least we thought we did, with a little prompting from our aunt.

This was the route my brothers wanted to take. Dissent was out of the question. Being the youngest sometimes had its disadvantages and this was definitely one such occasion. I did not know the long route to Granny's house.

I imagined falling off my bike halfway through the tunnel and thereafter being consumed by a horde of hungry rodents which would have enjoyed a small, pink, slightly sweaty boy for a late lunch. I was not unfamiliar with rats as there were always a few around the farm, but various cats, the shepherd's dog and the men on the farm kept the rat population down to penny numbers.

Here there was, so I believed, a whole tunnel full of them waiting in ambush. I did try to get between John and Willie so that they could protect me but they were too quick for such a ploy. So I closed my eyes as much as it was safe to do so and pedalled as hard as I could.

I never heard a squeak or saw a scurry in the darkness and in about three and a half seconds I was through to the other side with my heart pumping and my pulse racing.

I was still in that state a few minutes later when we sat down at Granny's to enjoy our second bottle of lemonade that day, only this time there were also helpings of scones filled with raspberry jam.

I do not recall the journey home in the back of the family car but Dad did say later that he had never had such a quiet, 'tired out' car load of passengers.

Misdemeanours and Punishment

THERE had been little outbreaks of misbehaviour at Flisk Primary school. At least, that is what the teacher Mrs Armstrong alleged. Even though I was now in primary four, I was not prepared to argue the point with her. It did not seem to me that a little talking in class was out of order, or that even the throwing of a pencil across the room to my friend David was much of an issue.

She was none too pleased another time when I experimented with making my chair squeak. If I leaned back, it gave a little squeak which stopped when I moved forward. It seemed to squeak more on one side of the chair than the other, which seemed to be almost squeak-free. I was enjoying myself with this experiment when, for no reason at all, I was given a row by the teacher.

The row did not worry me a great deal because I had already made up my mind that teachers seemed to concern themselves greatly about such trivial issues as speaking, squeaking and throwing things.

Mrs Armstrong said there needed to be a campaign to

improve the discipline in her school of twenty pupils. I was mentioned specifically, along with David, who had, incidentally, failed to catch the flying pencil but had bent down, picked it up and then thrown it back. Another pupil to gain a specific mention was my friend Ronnie whose regular seat was just in front of the teacher's desk. He was there so that she could keep an eye on him, she said.

The idea was that she would write up a 'code of good behaviour' on the blackboard and all the senior pupils, who included the main suspects, were to copy what she had written onto a large sheet of paper. Thus the school rules were transcribed, but not, as David whispered, onto 'tablets of stone.' I had already found out about the Ten Commandments when I went to Sunday school, but it was obvious that Mrs Armstrong had decided we needed a different set of 'thou shalt nots' within her classroom.

They were all rather tame, I thought, and they were all in the first person singular so that there was no escape by saying I did not understand that the rules applied to me. 'I shall not run about in the classroom' left little scope for avoidance. Similarly, 'I shall not speak during class lessons' was fairly direct and unequivocal. Lest these instructions might be forgotten, after they had been copied out, all the pupils had to pin them inside the lid of their desks. There they would be visible every time we opened our desk as we went for our jotters, pencils or even our play-break sandwich.

The unanswered question in our minds, or at least in mine, was what would happen if we transgressed. That thought occupied my mind for some considerable length of time until, that is, I decided to ask David what he thought would happen.

The answer came quickly, but not from the direction I had thought it would.

'Andrew, you will mark a black dot at the foot of the school rules and write alongside it: *speaking in class*.'

Putting a black dot and those few words was none too bad a penalty, but the next step in my learning experience was that three black dots at the foot of my behaviour sheet equalled a belting.

The older boys had told me that the teacher kept a leather strap inside her desk. Some of them had actually seen it. They said it was about three feet long and the leather had been cut at one end to create three prongs. One of the older boys said it actually had metal spikes in the end so that anyone who had received it ended up with bleeding hands. I soon found out he had been fibbing as there were no spikes on the end of it, but it still looked rather fearsome.

Eventually I had gained three black dots, so I was told to come to the front of the class and hold my crossed hands in front of me. I was not told to close my eyes tightly, but I did so because I still expected that blood would flow from where the belt hit and I did not fancy that.

So with eyes closed I missed the actual action. I did not ask for a replay as my hands were really stinging and my eyes were stinging just as badly. I was not going to cry because the whole school was watching. I think my friends wanted me to cry, and it was a close-run thing.

I was not the only one to be belted as David soon totted up the necessary number of black dots and he followed. I noticed that when the belt was about to hit his hands, he lowered them, which was a good tip to remember for the future as it seemed to lessen the stinging effect. Much later on, Ronnie actually dropped his hands altogether as the strap came down but that was not a good idea as the strap then hit the teacher's leg and she looked quite angry as she hopped about a bit on one leg before starting again with what seemed to be increased vigour and determination.

One day, the boys at school were sent out to dig the school garden and we thought this would be far away from any possible discipline. That is not the reason we started a fight by throwing divots of grass at each other, but if you have been hit with a piece of turf, you have to get revenge. The fight was going quite well when we heard a rattle on the classroom window above the garden. The teacher was shaking her fist and then she indicated, in rather a fierce way I thought, that she wanted all of us to come back into the classroom. I had not thought much about my name until that time, but when she said we should line up in alphabetical order to be belted, I wondered if it was too late to be called Zacharias.

The black dot system did not survive. By the time I was in primary five it had disappeared, but the same rules existed and the belt lay curled up in the teacher's desk, most of the time emerging only to restore discipline in the school.

Getting the belt was actually very helpful to me as I found out about things much earlier than some of my friends and especially the girls who never, ever seemed to be belted. One snowy day I was involved in tackling the primary six and seven pupils in a snowball fight. Some of the action took place rather close to the classroom with one badly thrown snowball crashing against a window. Even though it was still playtime, Mrs Armstrong came out with the belt slung over her shoulder almost, I thought, like some Western gunslinger that I had seen in one of my comics. The problem for me was that she was heading in my direction. I knew the routine, but what I did find out that day was that the effect of the belt was far, far worse when it hit cold, cold hands.

I do not remember who taught the school when I was in primary six. We had been told that Mrs. Armstrong had suffered a nervous breakdown. She returned the following year, but now she carried a stick with her. This was mostly to help with her walking, but it also simplified the punishment routine as she could take immediate action with the stick against any miscreant.

Despite my poor reports in my progress card, Mrs Armstrong decided on an exit strategy. That is, her strategy on my exit from her school. She must have reckoned life would be easier if I went off to secondary school. Like everyone else, I had to sit the 'eleven plus' exam and, as Mrs Armstrong was taking no chances of my remaining at school, I was kept behind for extra lessons. I did not like that, but then she fed me fish which she said helped my brains and that was not so bad as I knew I would also get my tea when I went home.

The exam was not too bad, even if it was strange to have to sit and answer a lot of questions which seemed to have little to do with all of the things I was interested in, such as football and tractors.

After the summer holidays, I arrived at the 'big' school in Cupar where, within a few days, I found out I was by far the youngest pupil at secondary school.

Gina, my smaller sister, was still at Flisk school and one night not long after the new term started, she told Mum and Dad it was now much quieter with her big brother no longer there.

Two Views from a Window

MY friends have all wandered off and left me sitting on this big stone by the roadside, thinking my thoughts. I can see them along the road at the Big Den, where a stream comes down the hill and runs alongside the road. At this time of year, you can see sticklebacks and little fishes in the water. John said he once saw a trout and although no one else believed him I would always stick up for my big brother.

I know my friends will stop at the water – but they will not play in it because it comes down from the hill and is very cold. It will not be difficult to catch them up. I am quite good at running and I wonder about hiding my schoolbag in the hedge and then collecting it in the morning. That would allow me to run much faster. However I do not consider this for long because I foresee questions from Mum about homework. In any case, I will need my bag tomorrow to carry my school piece which I hope will be filled with jam and not cheese which I have had three times this week.

I stand up from where I have been sitting and thinking of all the fun and games I have had. Everyone knows that there are only sixty seconds in each minute but there are so many things to do that sometimes I wish we had bigger minutes. Maybe not in school, though, as the minutes there are long enough already.

I look back to the cottage and peer through the window at the old man still sitting there in his chair. His head has drooped forward and it seems as if he has fallen asleep. I was enjoying telling him my tales. Old people are like that. They often ask you things and then when you are telling them they either fall asleep or else they ask you a silly question such as, 'Have you washed your hands before you have your meal?' or 'Have you done your homework?' They know you haven't but they still ask.

Perhaps now the old man is no longer listening I will just sneak away because there are so many things I still have to do. . . .

My eyes have closed but I am not asleep. I am thinking warm thoughts of days long gone. The ones I am remembering are the happy ones, the ones where there were fun and laughter.

Sometimes, I do remember the sad times when people fell ill and died, or when accidents happened and people were injured. I recall, too, Mum and Dad talking about wars and battles after they listened to the news.

I look up and see the river. The tide is slowly ebbing out, revealing sand and mud banks. The ruins of the castle are still as they were fifty years ago but the school is closed and the classroom is now part of a house. The farm is still there but it is different and quiet for most of the year as there are no gangs of children playing around the yard and seldom any men working in the fields.

My friends at school have all grown up and the winds that guide people's lives have blown them away from this little parish.

About the Author

ANDREW Arbuckle comes from a Fife farming family which, like many others, could trace its roots back to the west of Scotland. The third son of a tenant farmer, Andrew went on to farm with his father in the 1970s. The farm was mainly arable, growing malting barley, seed potatoes and, before the closure of the local refining factory, sugar beet. The tenancy of the farm was given up in the late 1980s.

During his farming, Andrew contributed to a number of farming magazines and this interest developed into full-time agricultural journalism with the Dundee *Courier* where he was farming editor for fifteen years.

A short spell as a member of the Scottish Parliament followed between 2005 and 2007. Over the past twenty years, he has been a councillor in Fife. Nowadays, he is a freelance journalist combining this with agricultural public relations work.

He has two grown-up daughters, one a solicitor and the other a psychiatrist.

Andrew has also written *Footsteps in the Furrow*, a commentary on Scottish farming life from 1900 to the present day. To create this account, Andrew gathered information from a variety of sources, such as newspaper archives, union meeting minutes and interviews with those who lived and worked on the farms, giving his account of farming heritage a rich vitality.

Other Books from Old Pond Publishing

Footsteps in the Furrow   ANDREW ARBUCKLE

A record of farming life in Scotland, from 1900 to the present day, by an author keenly aware of his own farming heritage. Andrew has gathered sources from newspaper archives, interviews and more. Paperback

Farmer's Boy   MICHAEL HAWKER

Michael Hawker's detailed recollections of work on North Devon Farms in the 1940s and 1950s. Paperback

Farming Day by Day – the 1960s   JOHN WINTER

This selection from John Winter's reports in the *Daily Mail* vividly recalls the ups and downs of a decade when Britain's farmers were still being encouraged to produce more food. Hardback

Country Dance   HENRY BREWIS

Based in Northumberland, this grimly humorous fable from the 1990s tells the story of a hill farmer selling up and his farm being 'developed'. Paperback

Clarts and Calamities   HENRY BREWIS

The fictional diary of a year in the life of a Northumbrian hill farmer: 'the daily scribbling of an umpteenth-generation peasant'. Paperback

The Rural World of Eric Guy   JONATHAN BROWN

From the 1930s to the 1960s Eric Guy photographed the downland farming scene around his Berkshire base. Jonathan Brown has selected 174 of his most striking photographs and provides a knowledgeable text. Paperback

Free complete catalogue:

Old Pond Publishing Ltd, Dencora Business Centre,
36 White House Road, Ipswich IP1 5LT,
United Kingdom

Secure online ordering: **www.oldpond.com**
Phone: 01473 238200